BEST OF LENNY BREAU

12 ESSENTIAL TRANSCRIPTIONS FROM THE LEGENDRY JAZZ GUITARIST

RECORDED VERSIONS GUITAR

AUTHENTIC TRANSCRIPTIONS
WITH NOTES AND TABLATURE

Cover photo by Jon Sievert/
Michael Ochs Archives/Getty Images

Music transcriptions by
Jeff Jacobson and Paul Pappas

ISBN 978-1-4950-0961-0

HAL•LEONARD®
CORPORATION

7777 W. BLUEMOUND RD. P.O. BOX 13819 MILWAUKEE, WI 53213

Visit Hal Leonard Online at
www.halleonard.com

from *The Velvet Touch of Lenny Breau - Live!*

Bluesette

Words by Norman Gimbel
Music by Jean Thielemans

*Chord symbols reflect overall harmony.

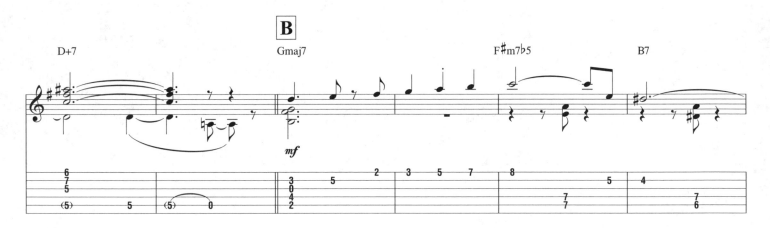

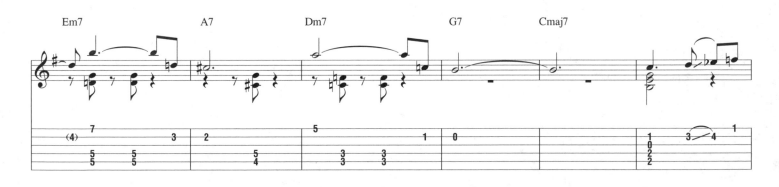

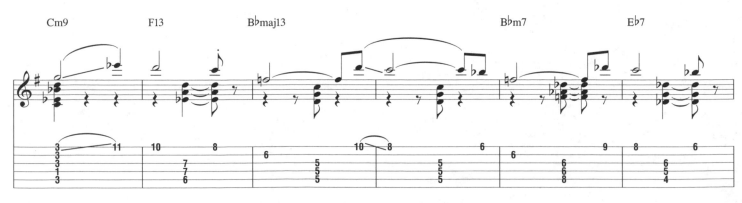

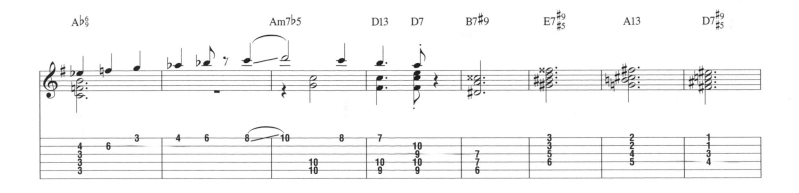

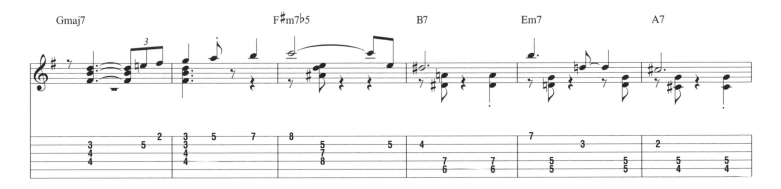

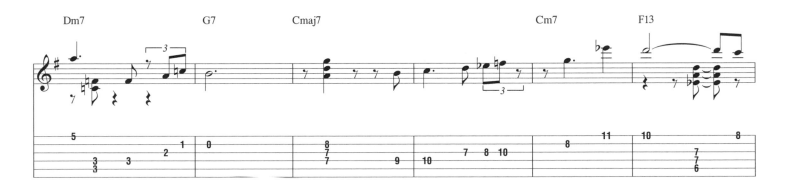

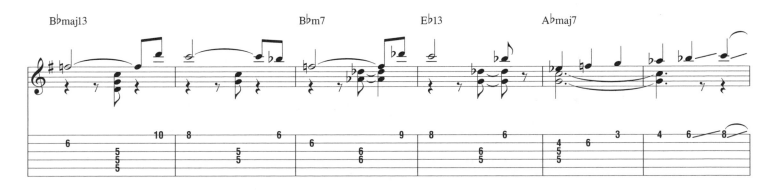

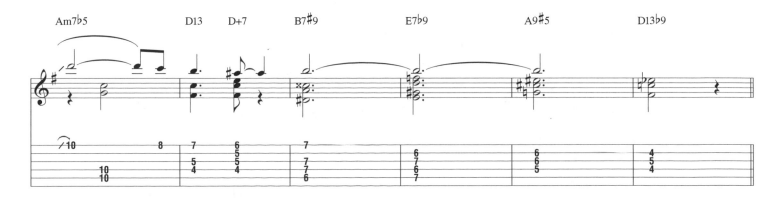

C

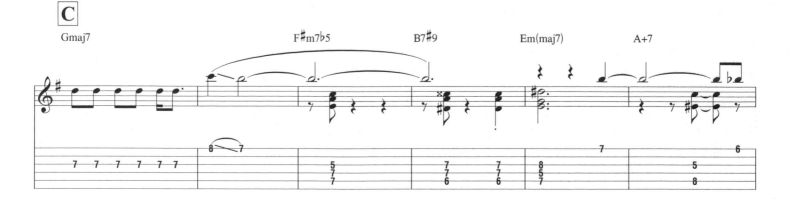

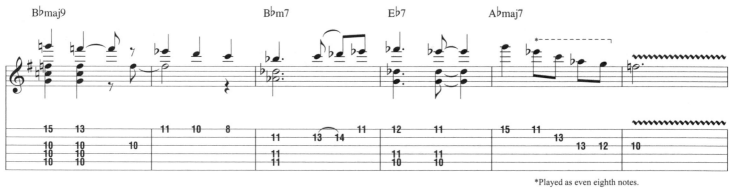

*Played as even eighth notes.

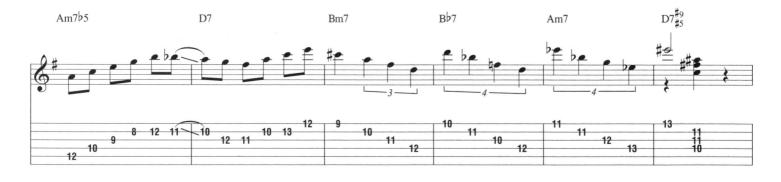

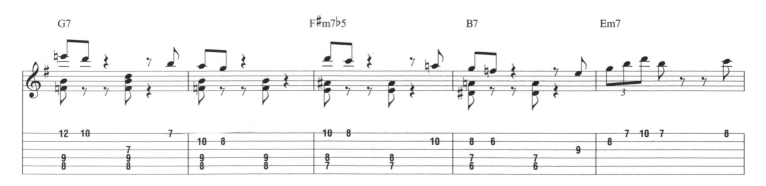

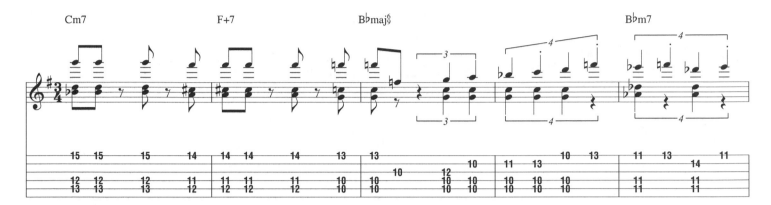

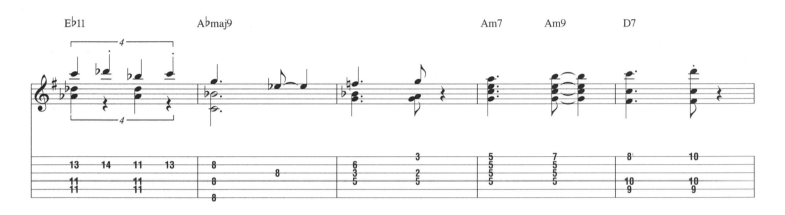

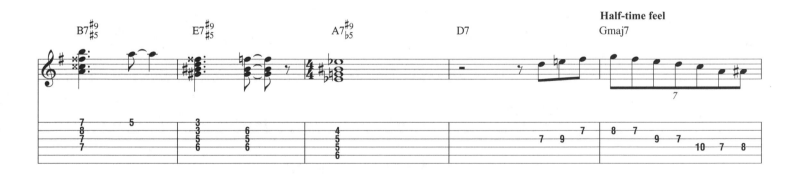

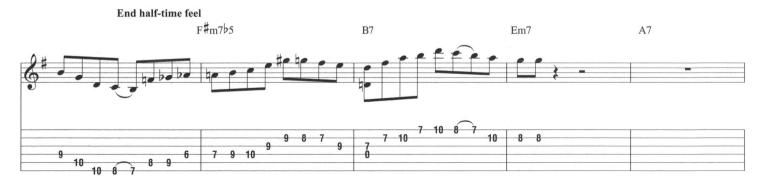

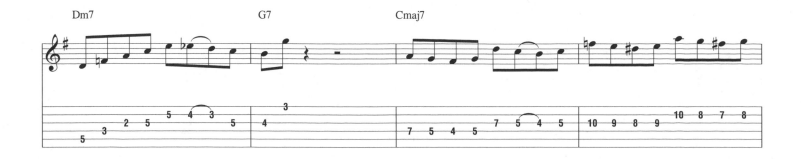

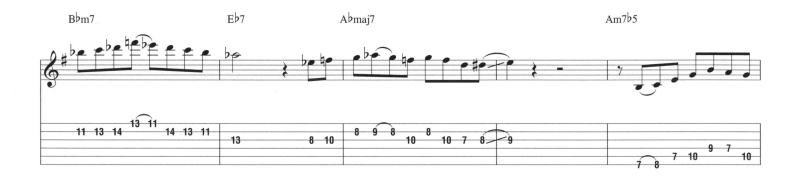

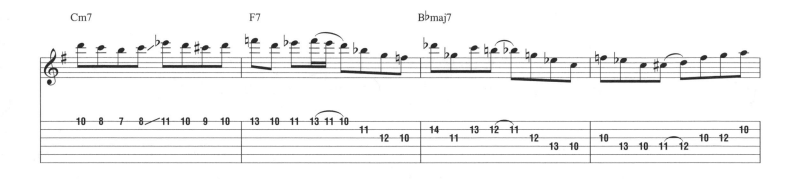

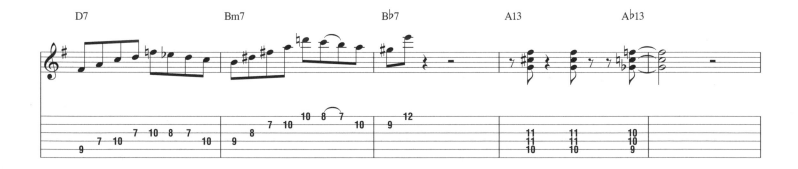

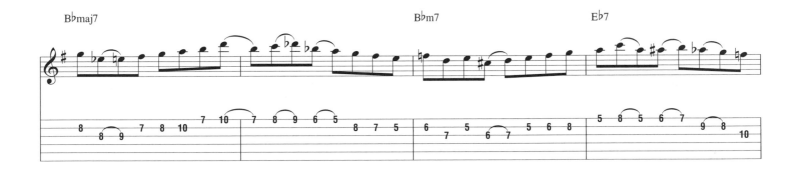

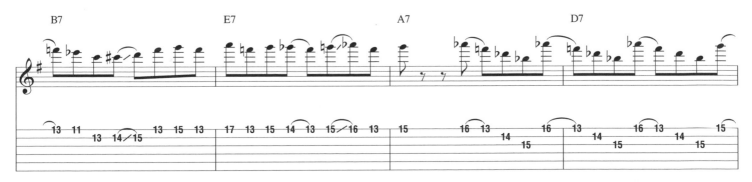

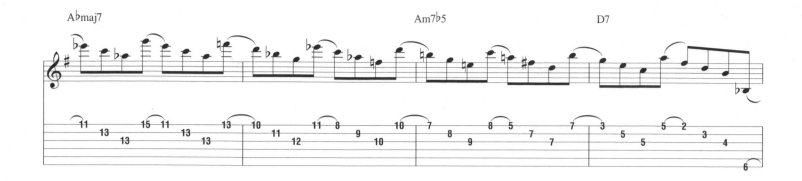

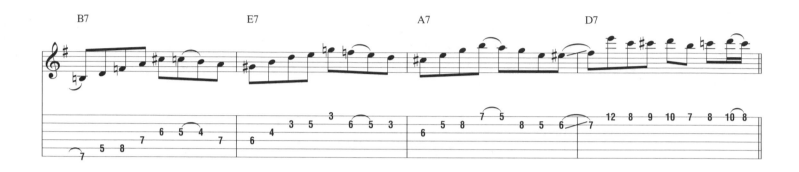

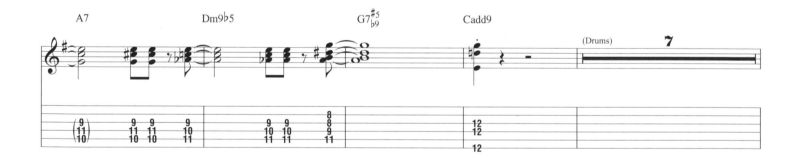

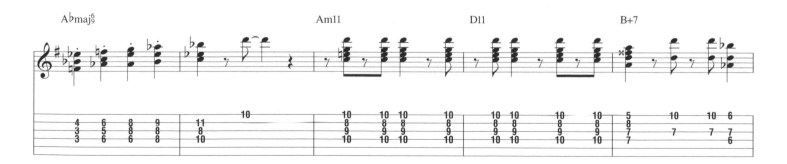

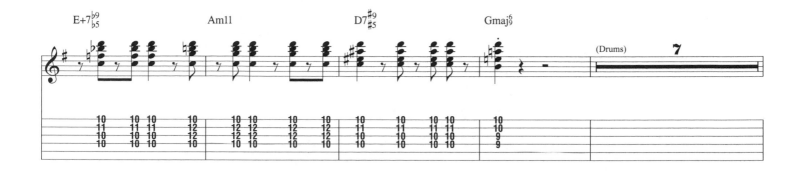

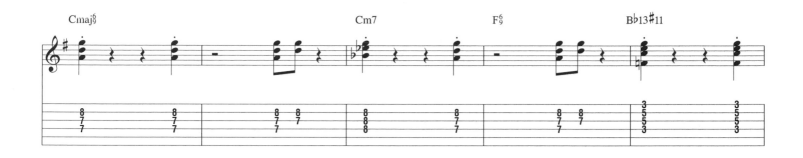

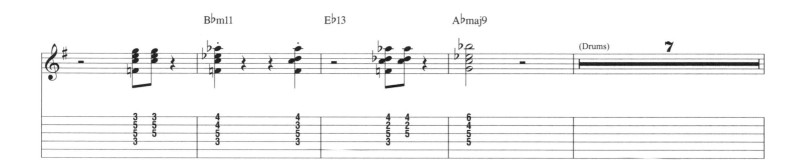

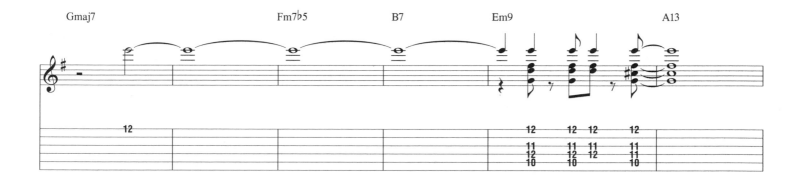

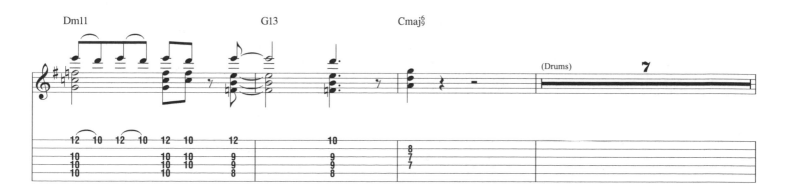

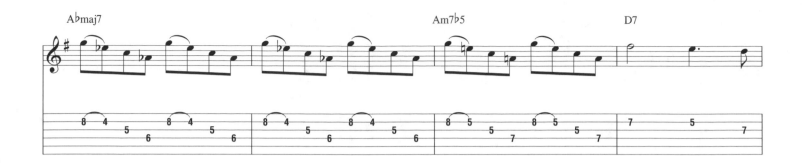

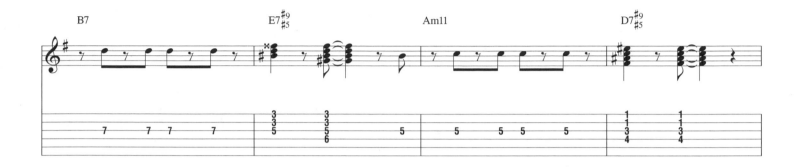

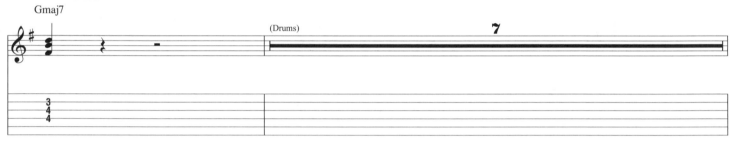

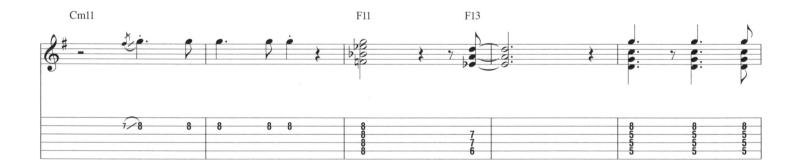

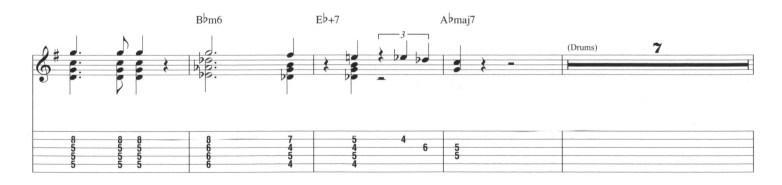

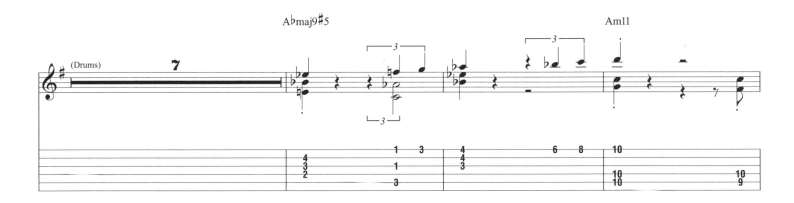

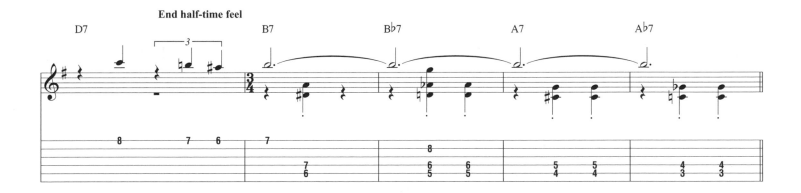

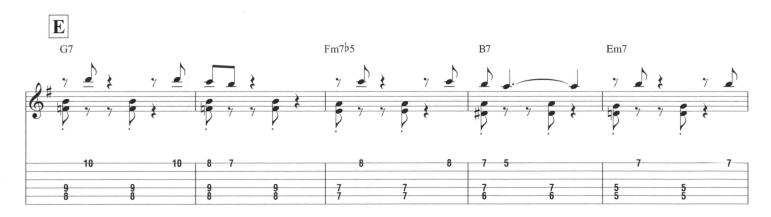

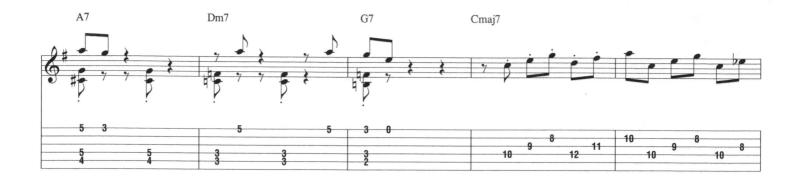

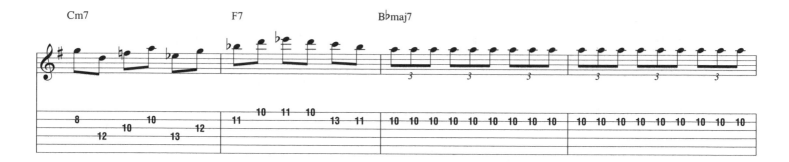

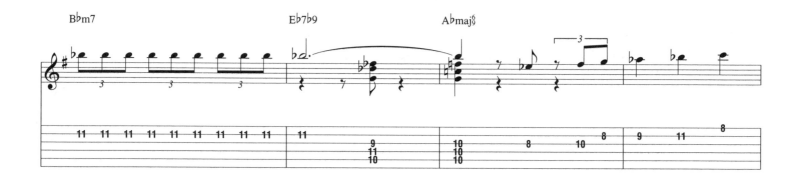

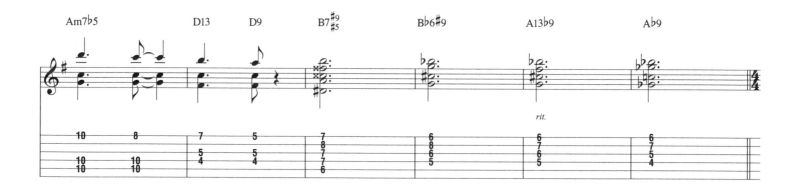

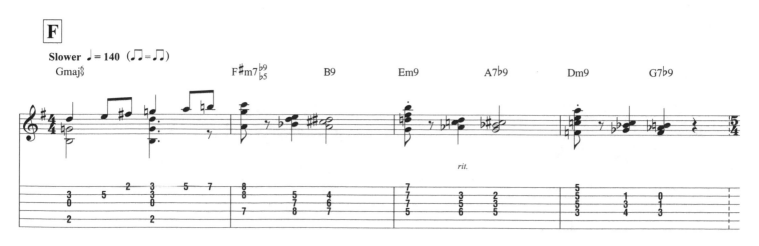

Free time

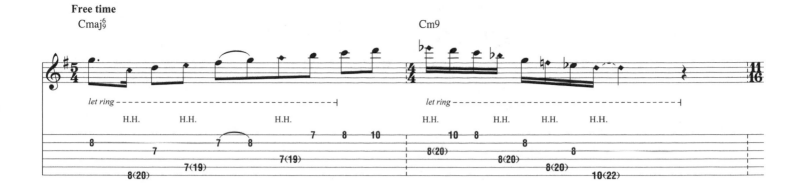

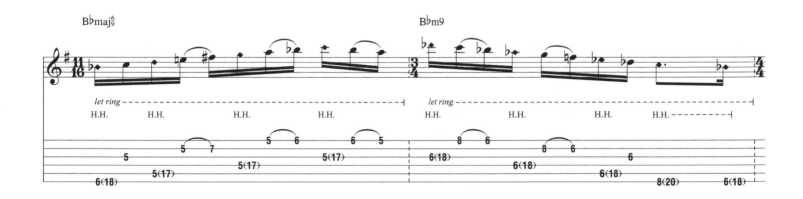

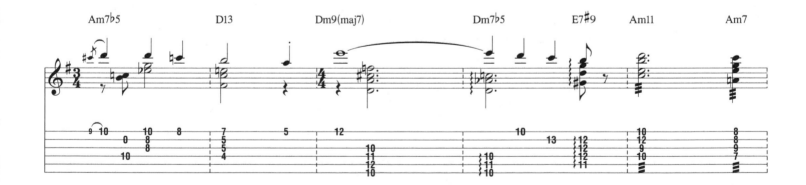

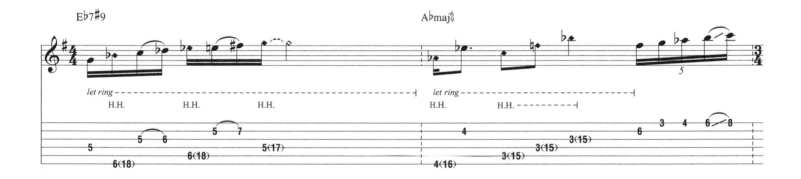

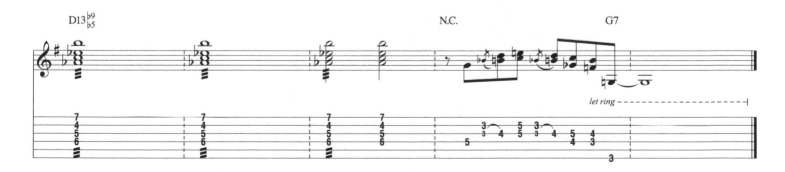

from *The Hallmark Sessions*

Cannon Ball Rag

By Merle Travis

A

Moderately ♩ = 110

*Chord symbols reflect implied harmony.
**P.M. applies to 4th, 5th & 6th strings only throughout.

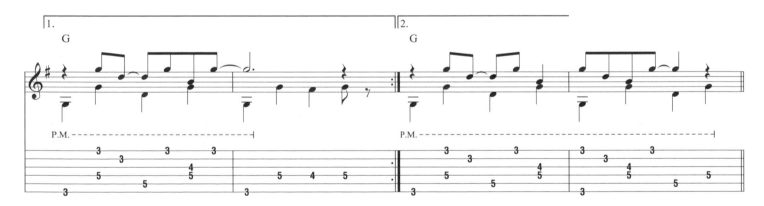

B

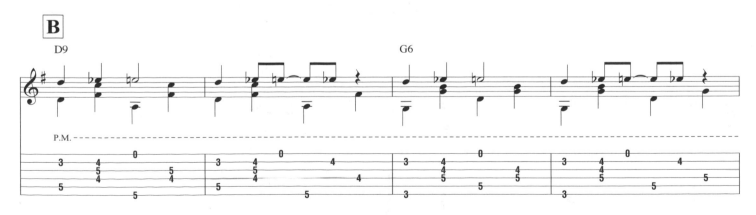

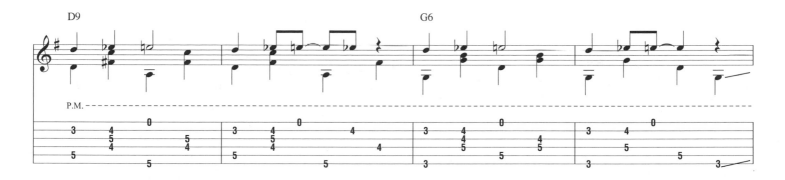

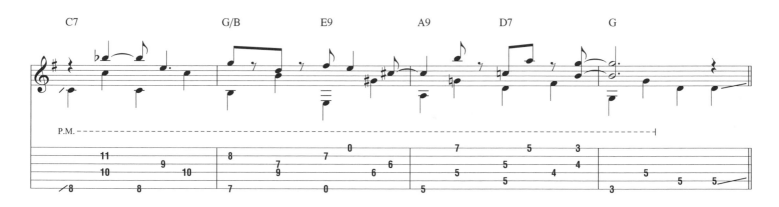

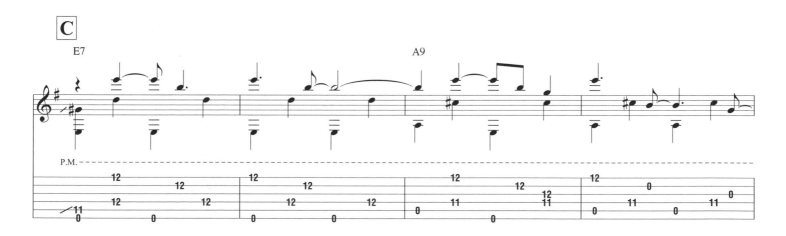

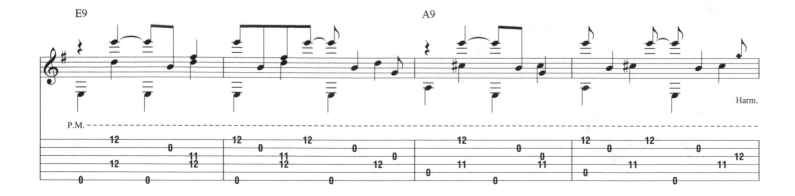

D

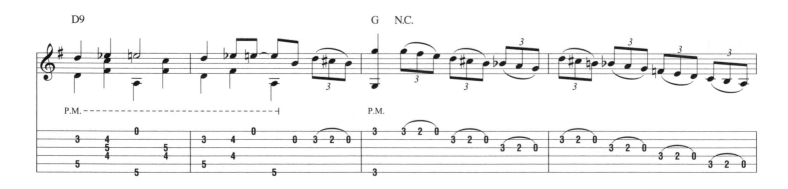

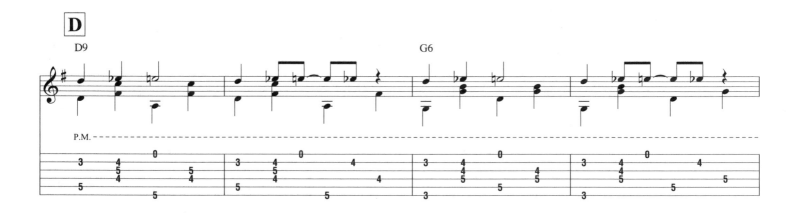

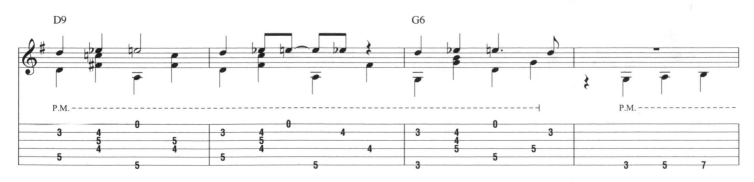

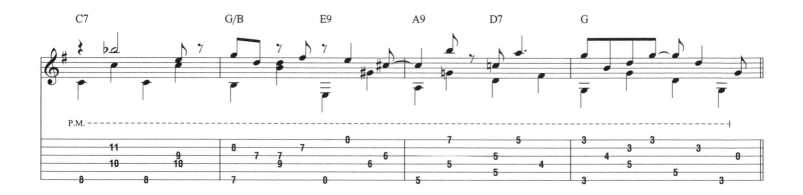

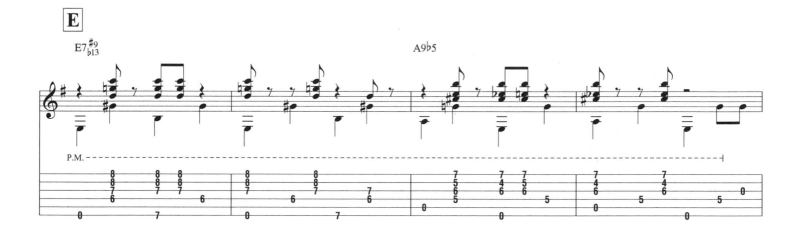

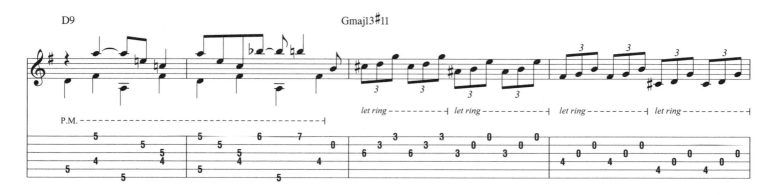

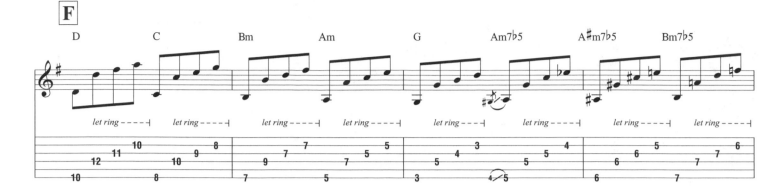

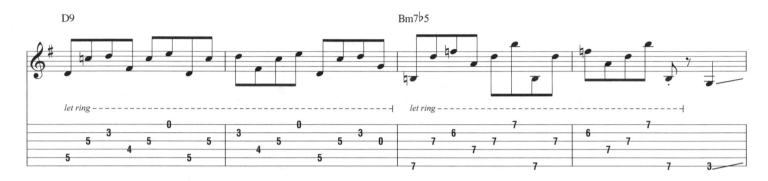

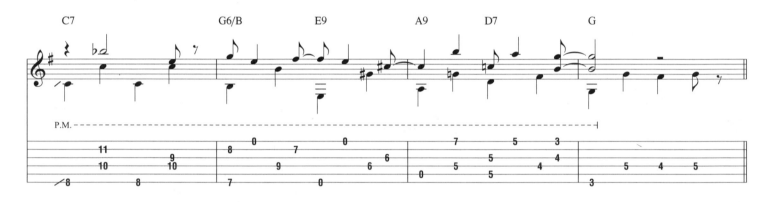

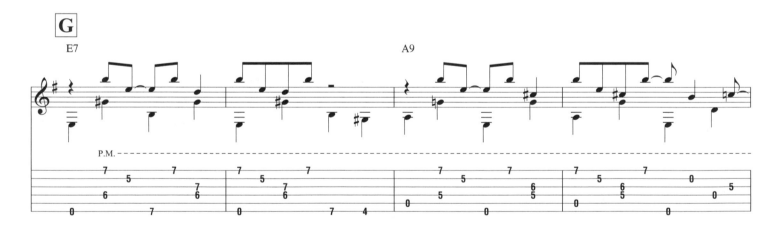

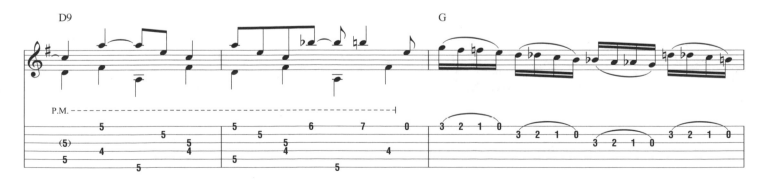

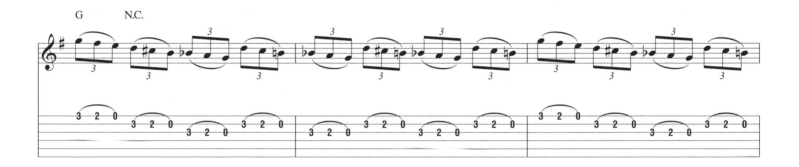

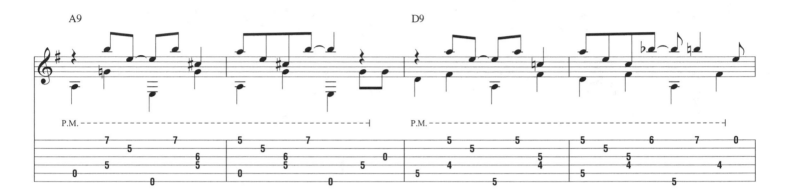

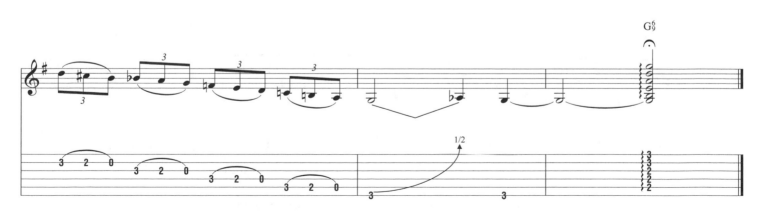

from *The Velvet Touch of Lenny Breau - Live!*

The Claw

By Jerry Reed

Capo II

*Symbols in parentheses represent chord names respective to capoed guitar.
Symbols above reflect actual sounding chords. Capoed fret is "0" in tab.
Chord symbols reflect implied harmony.

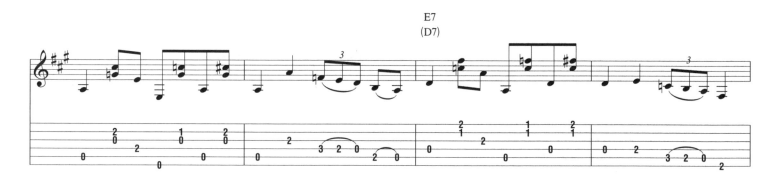

To Coda ⊕

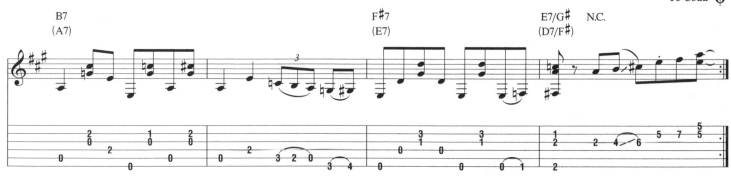

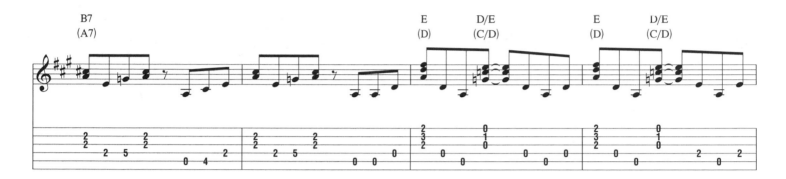

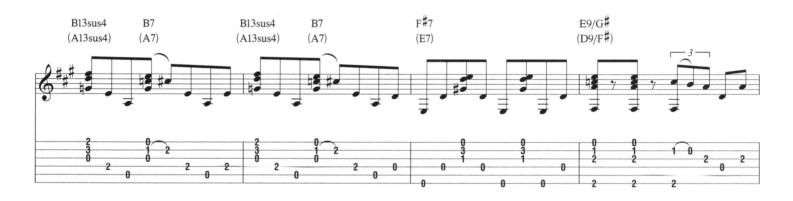

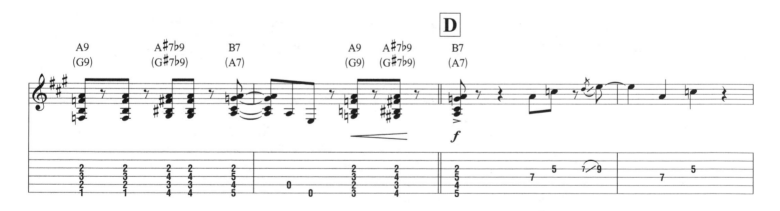

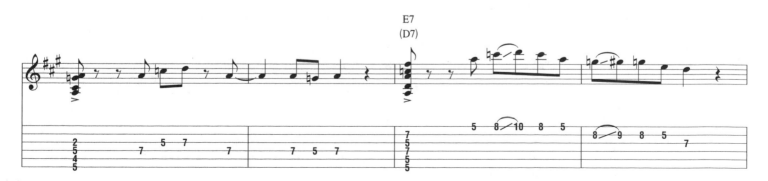

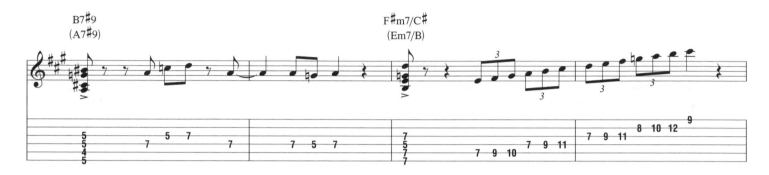

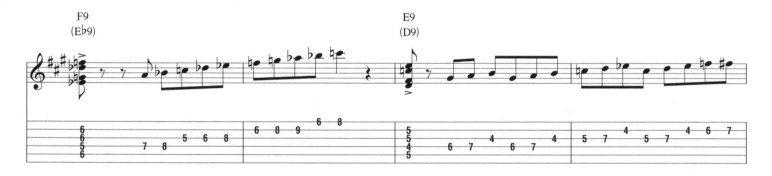

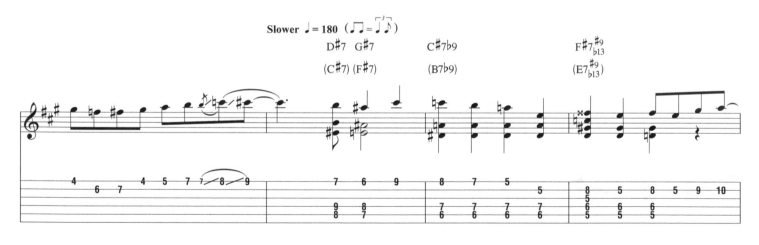

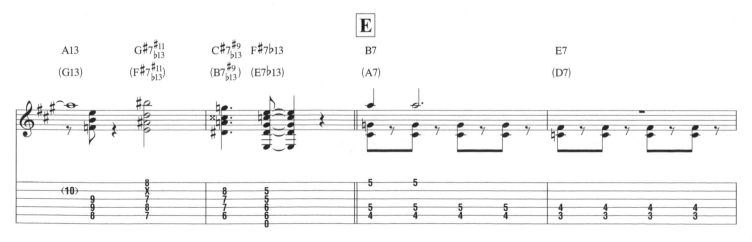

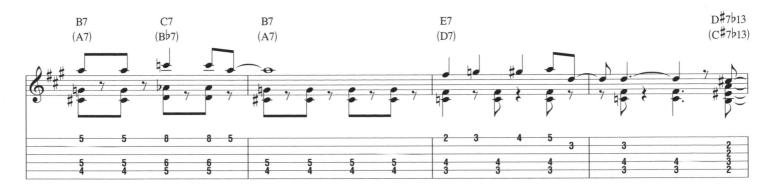

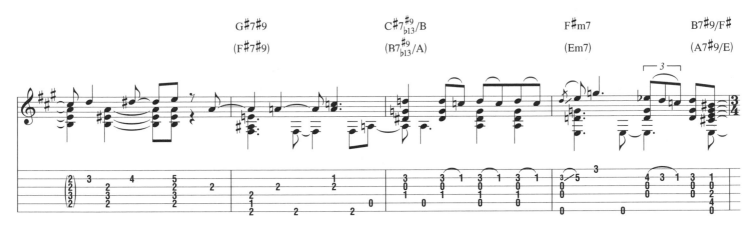

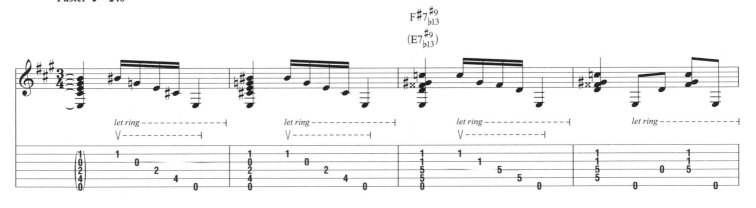

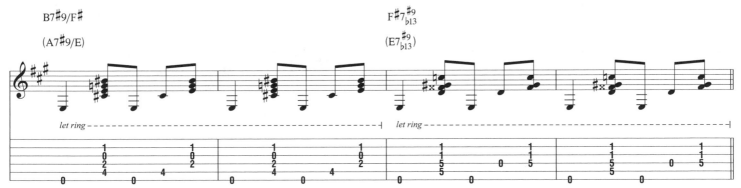

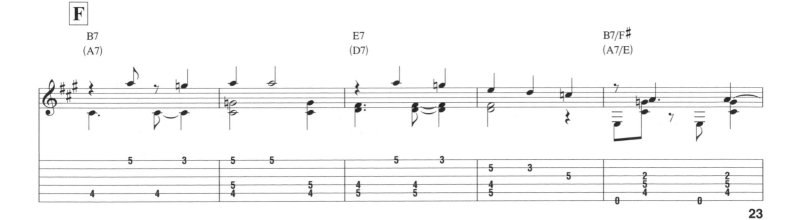

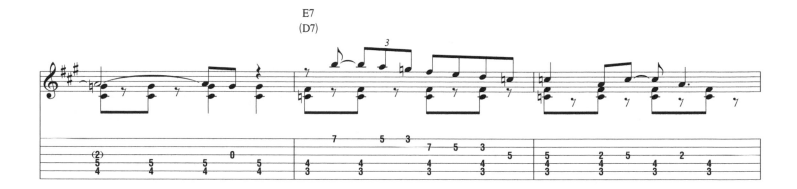

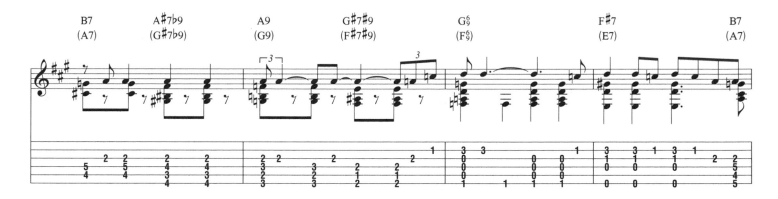

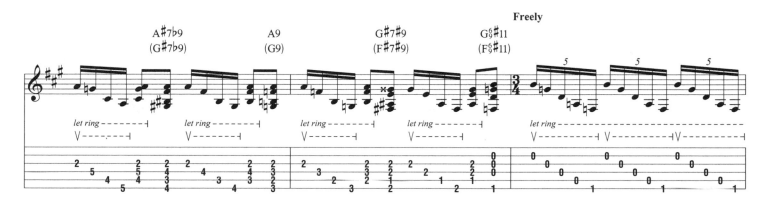

Faster ♩ = 252

Spoken: One, two, three, four, five, six. One, two, three, four, five.

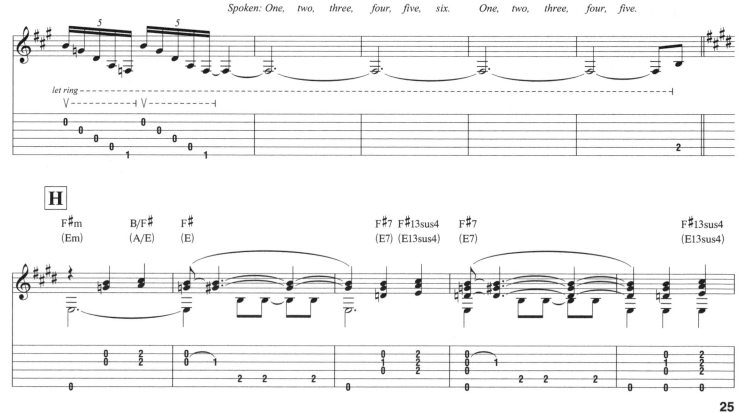

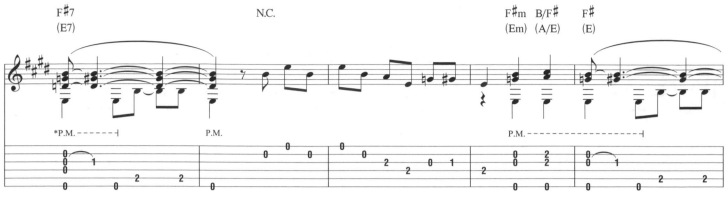

*P.M. refers to downstemmed notes only.

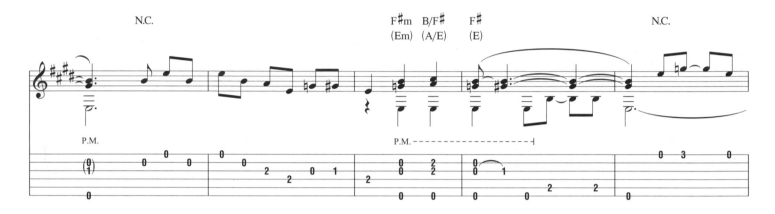

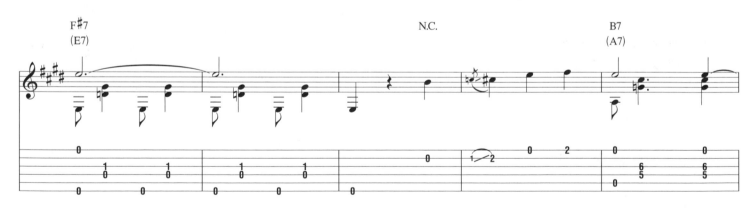

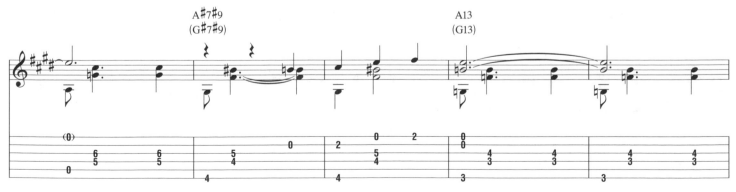

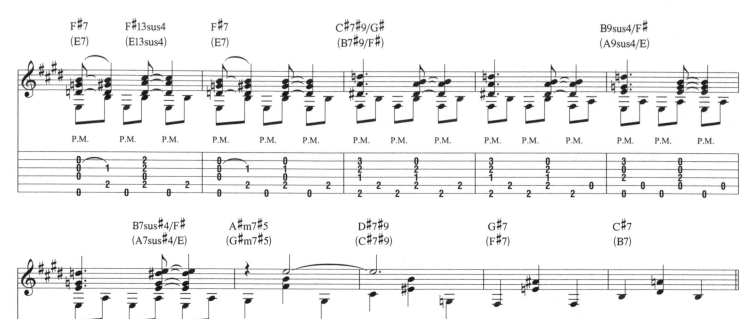

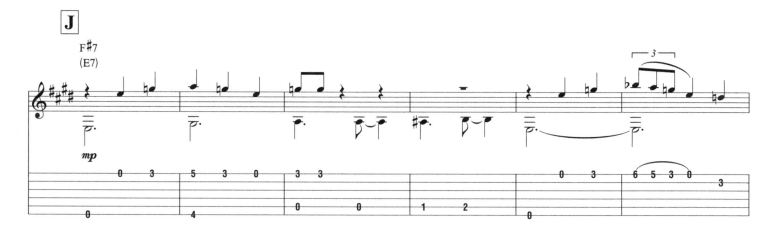

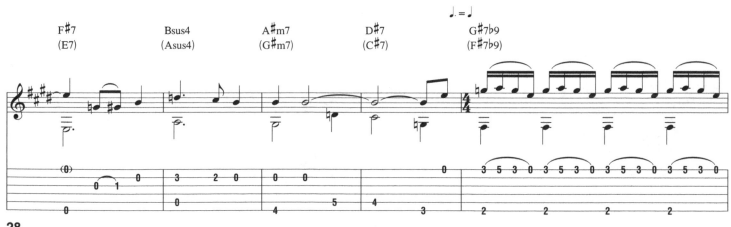

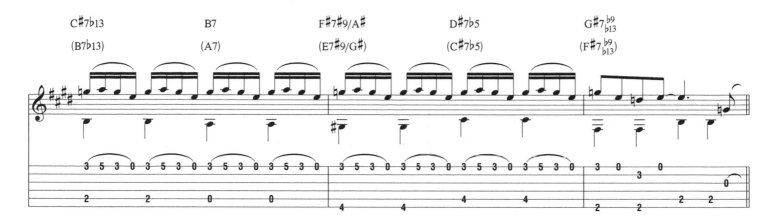

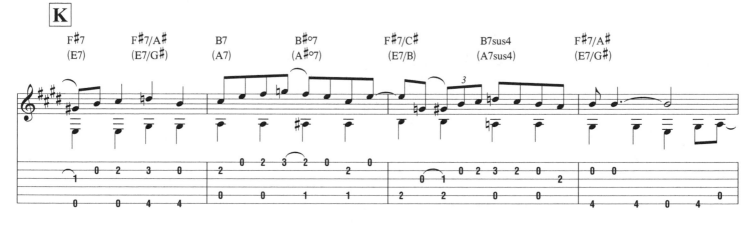

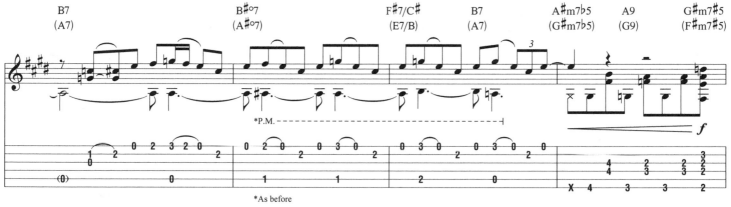

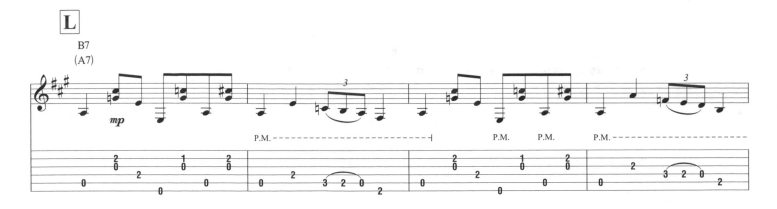

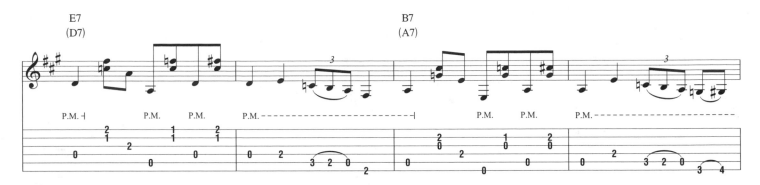

*P.M. on 6th string only.

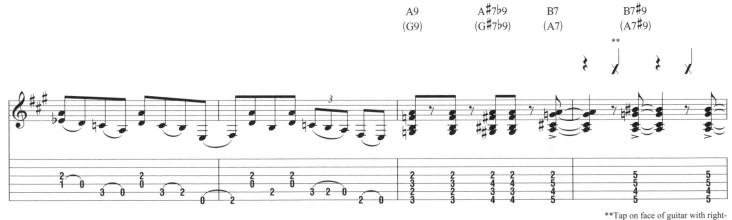

**Tap on face of guitar with right-hand fingers in specified rhythm.

Free time

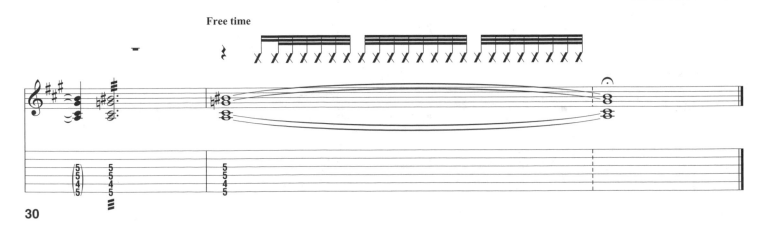

from *Five O'Clock Bells*

Days of Wine and Roses

Lyrics by Johnny Mercer
Music by Henry Mancini

Spoken: How's it feel?

Lenny, it sounds good.

*Tape splice

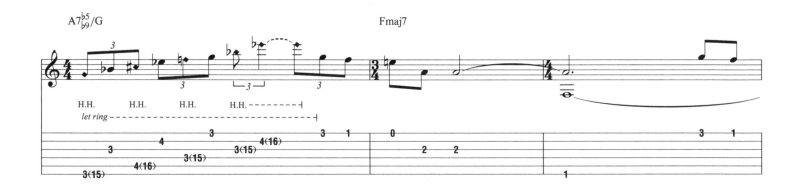

B

Gtr. 1 tacet

N.C.   C   Fmaj9   Em11

Gtr. 2 (elec.)

mp
w/ clean tone
w/ fingers

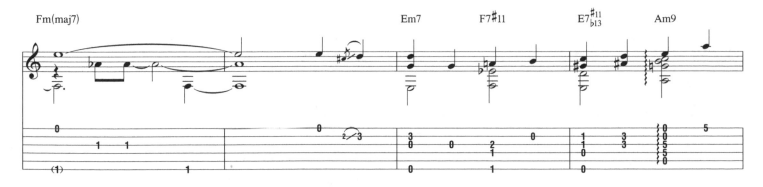

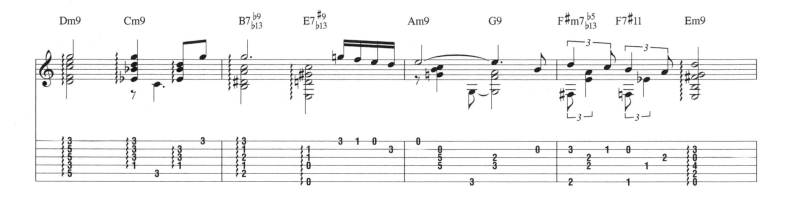

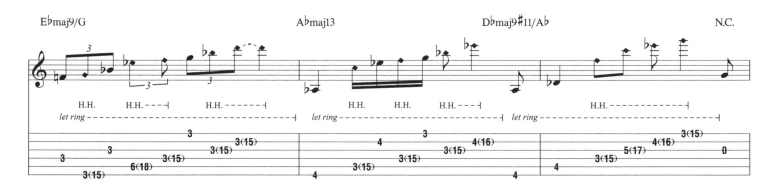

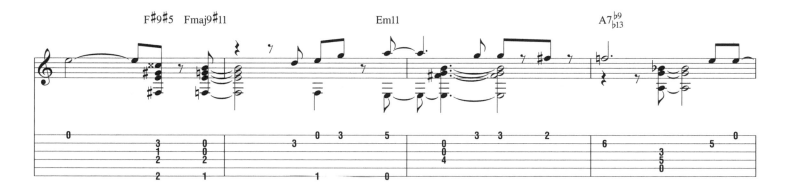

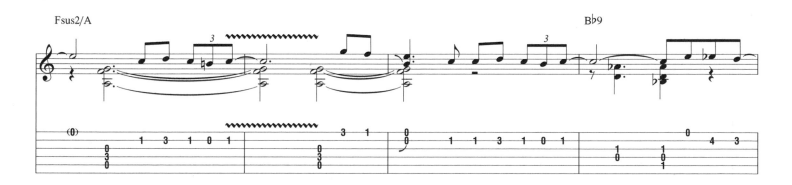

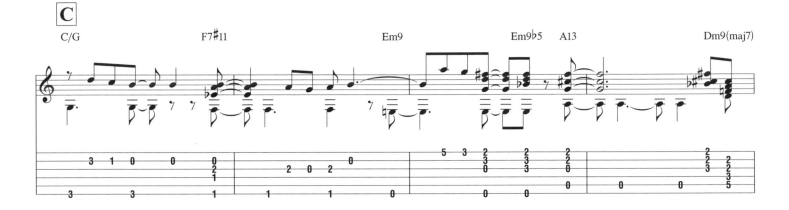

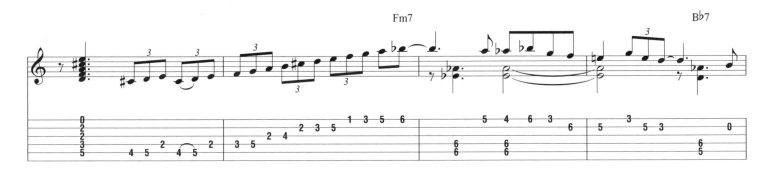

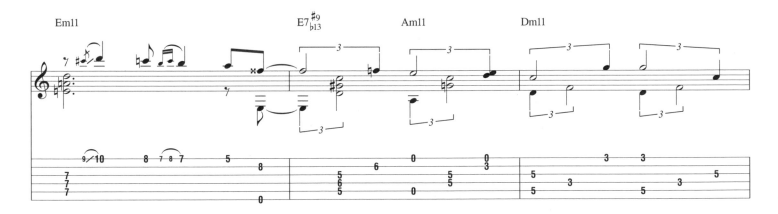

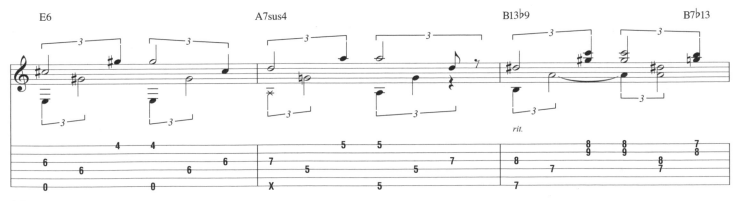

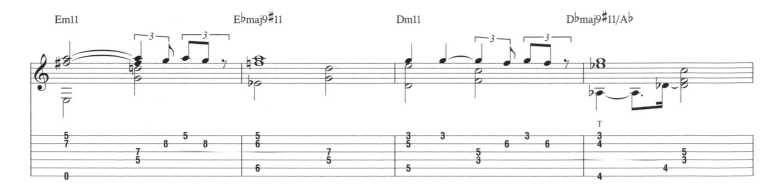

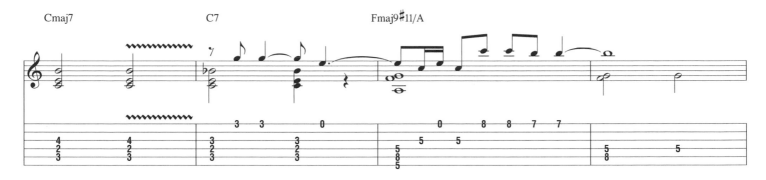

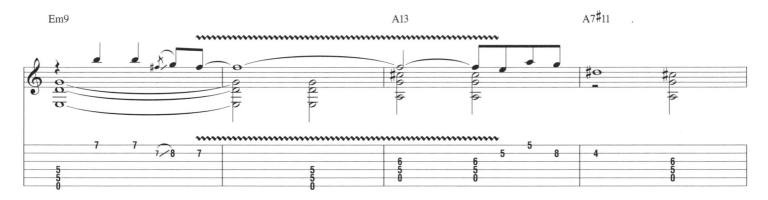

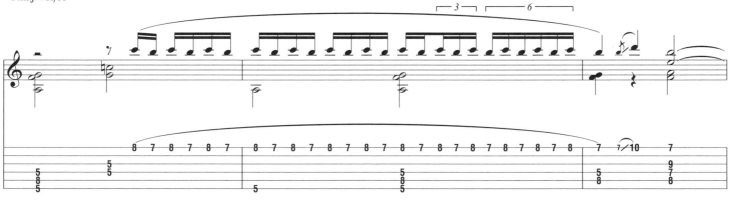

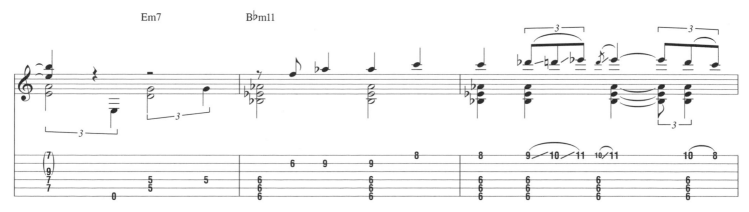

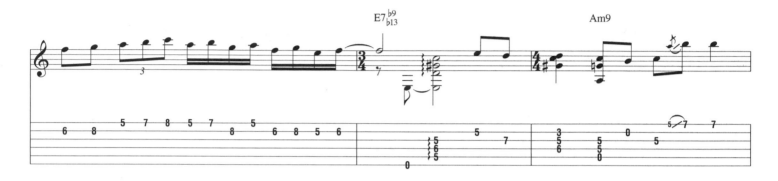

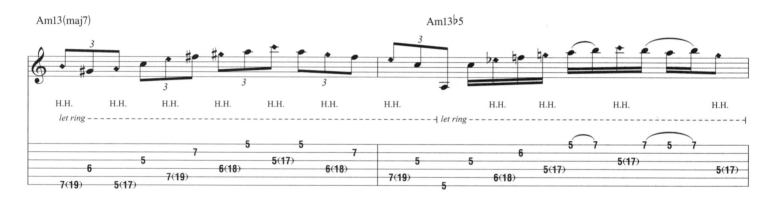

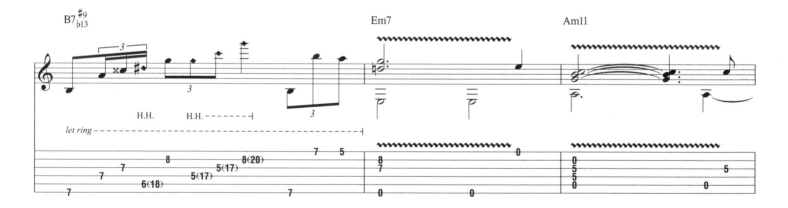

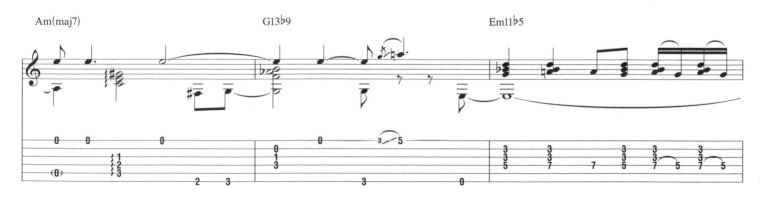

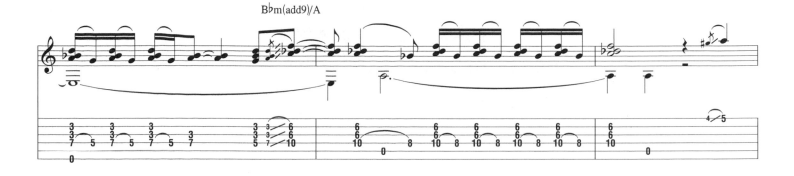

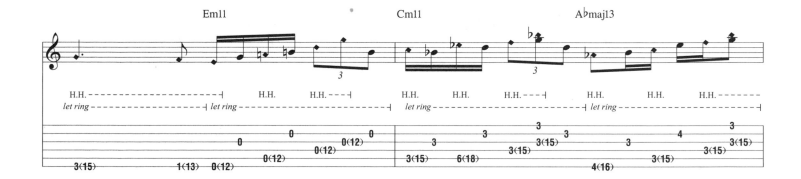

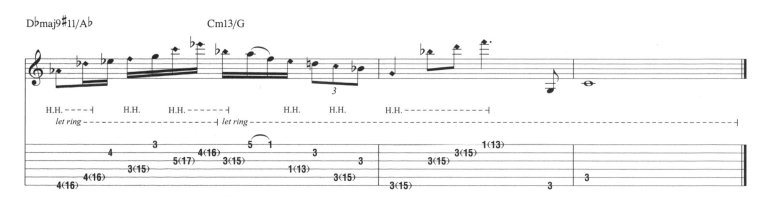

from *Guitar Sounds from Lenny Breau*

Freight Train

Words and Music by Paul James and Fred Williams

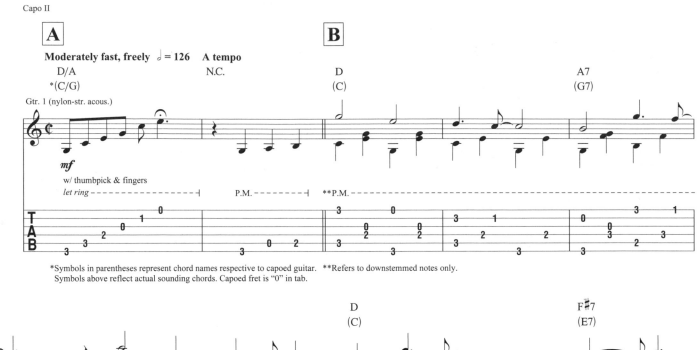

*Symbols in parentheses represent chord names respective to capoed guitar. **Refers to downstemmed notes only.
Symbols above reflect actual sounding chords. Capoed fret is "0" in tab.

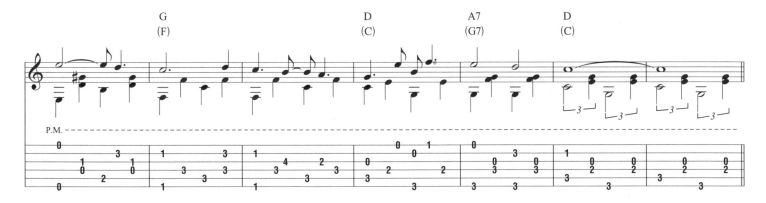

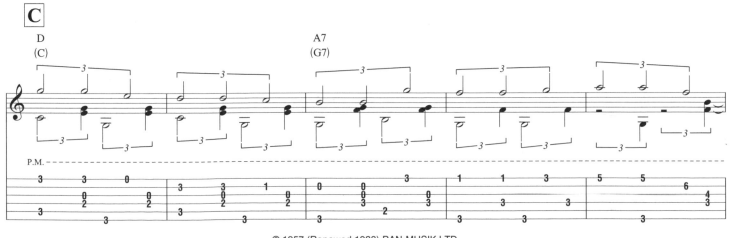

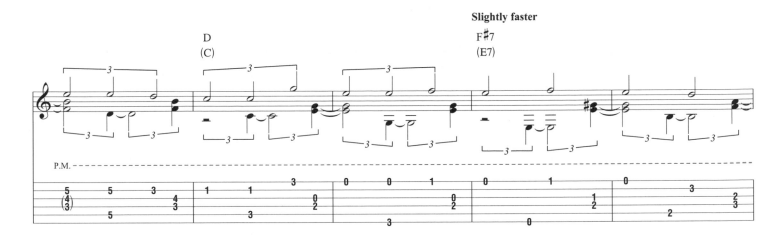

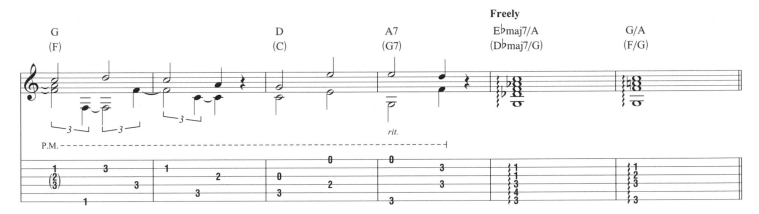

D

Tempo I

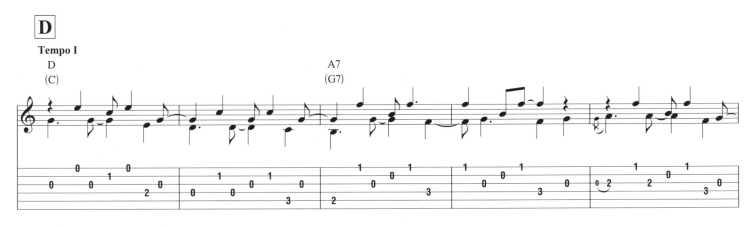

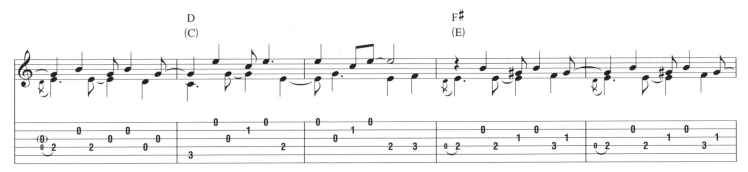

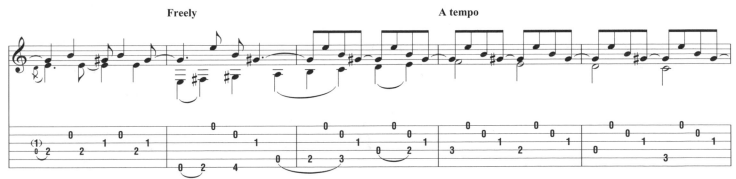

*Vib. refers to 2nd string only.

**Fret each adjacent set of strings w/ 1 finger.

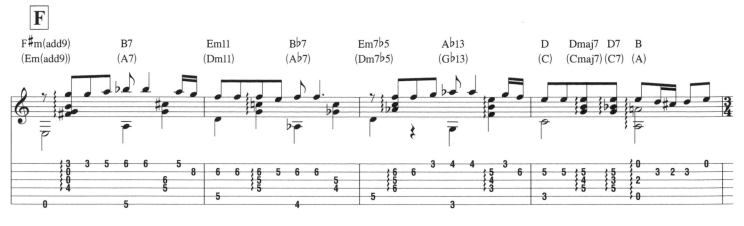

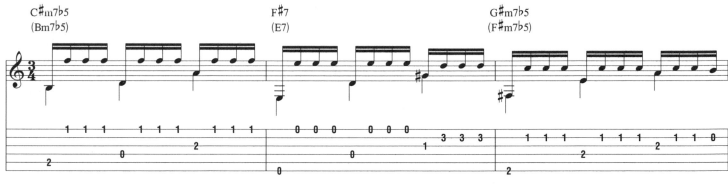

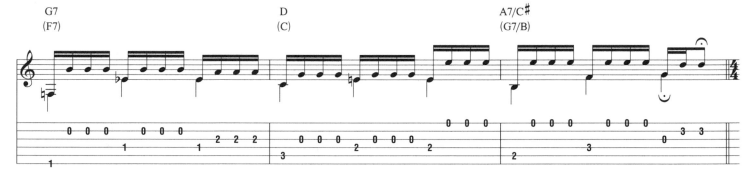

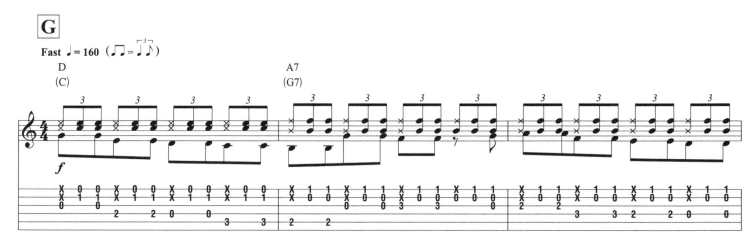

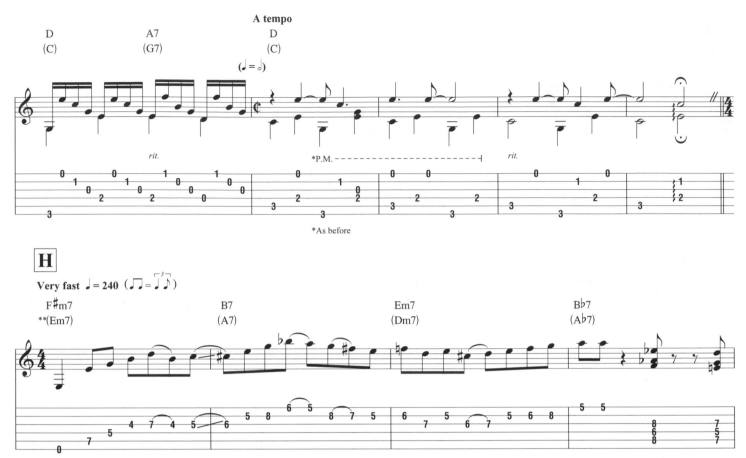

A tempo

*As before

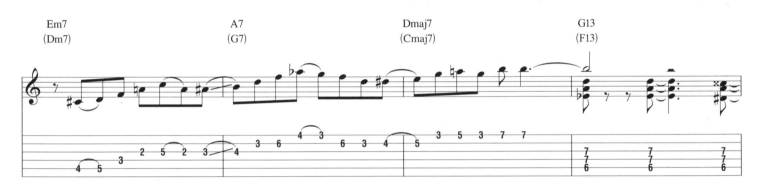

H

Very fast ♩ = 240 (♫ = ♪³♪)

**Chord symbols reflect implied harmony.

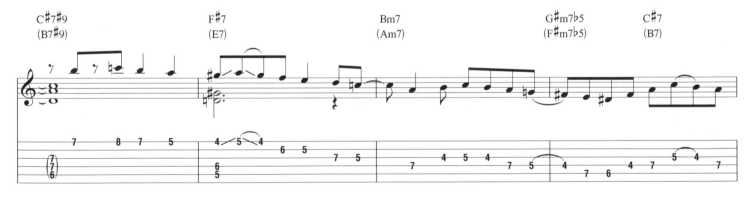

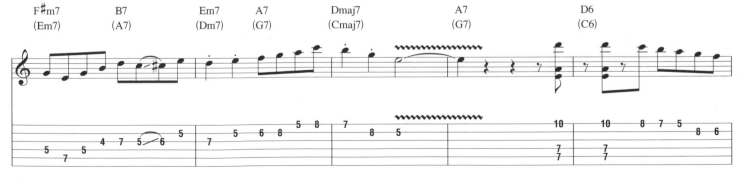

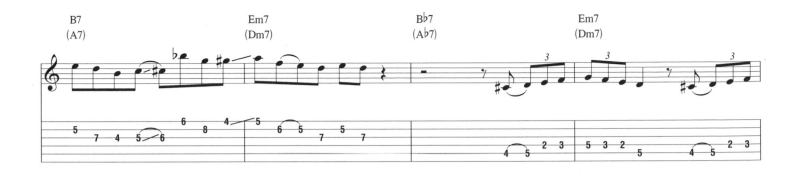

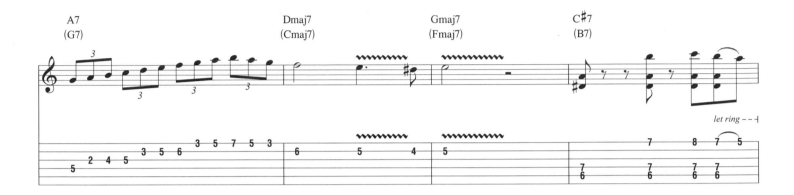

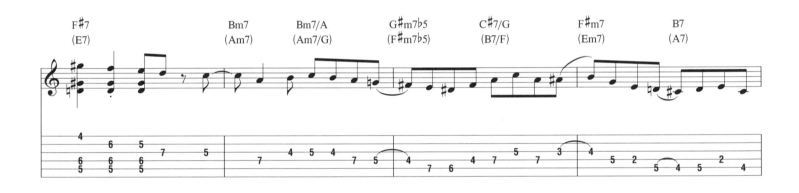

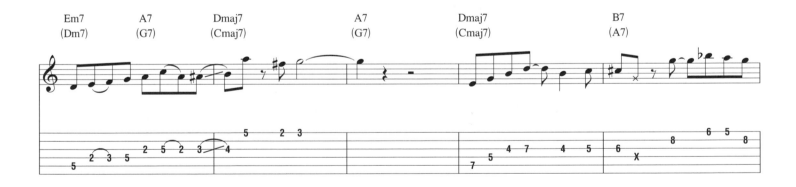

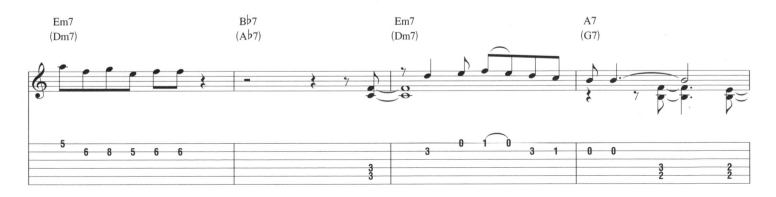

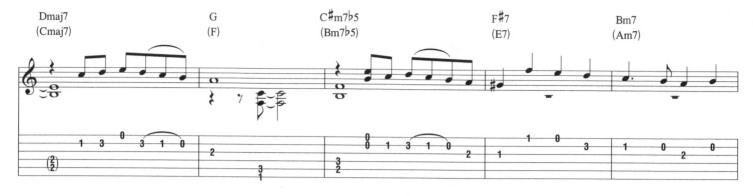

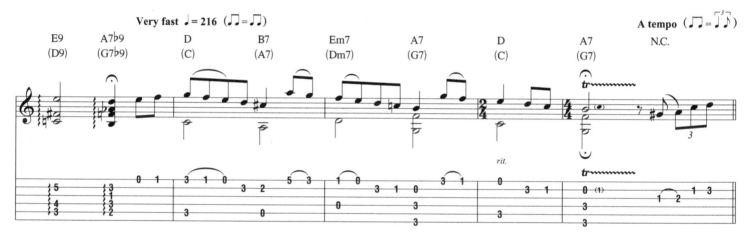

I

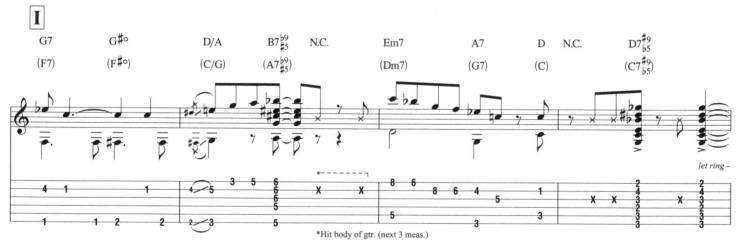

*Hit body of gtr. (next 3 meas.)

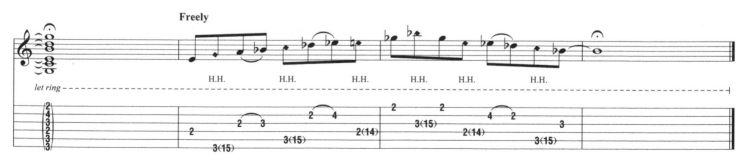

from *Guitar Sounds from Lenny Breau*

Georgia on My Mind

Words by Stuart Gorrell
Music by Hoagy Carmichael

*Chord symbols reflect overall harmony.

**Applies to 5th & 4th strings only.

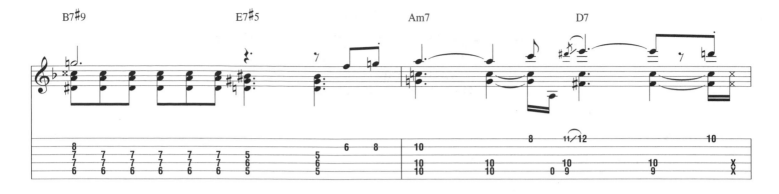

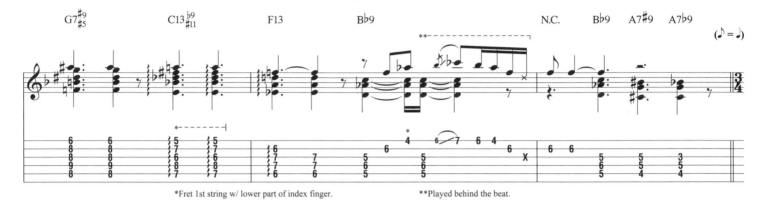

*Fret 1st string w/ lower part of index finger. **Played behind the beat.

D

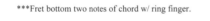

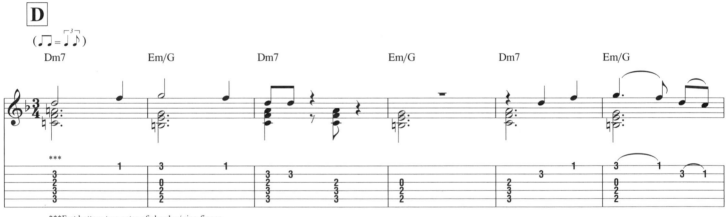

***Fret bottom two notes of chord w/ ring finger.

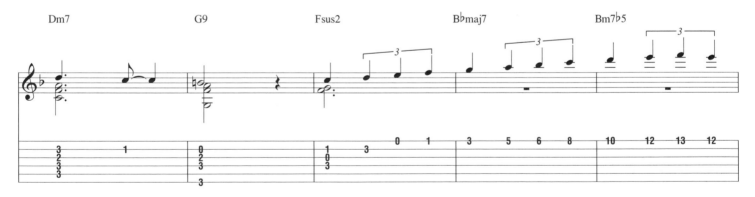

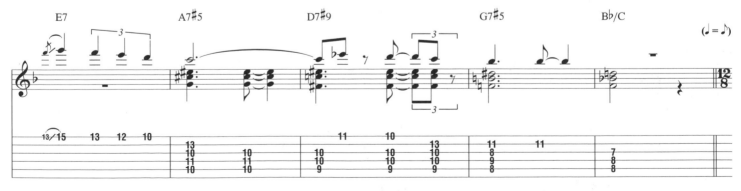

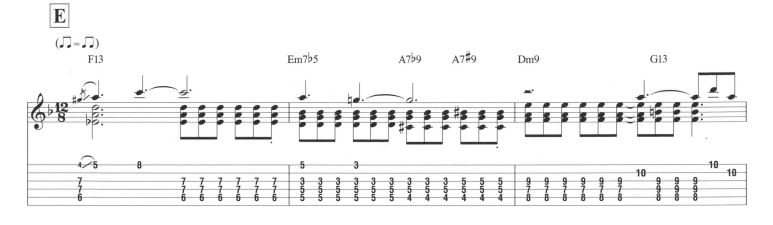

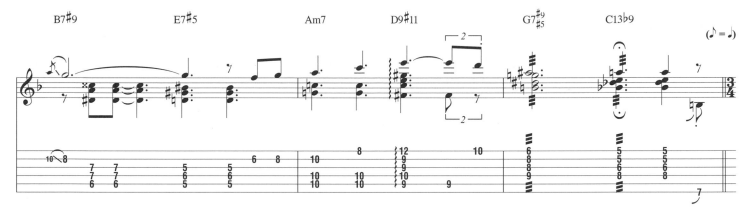

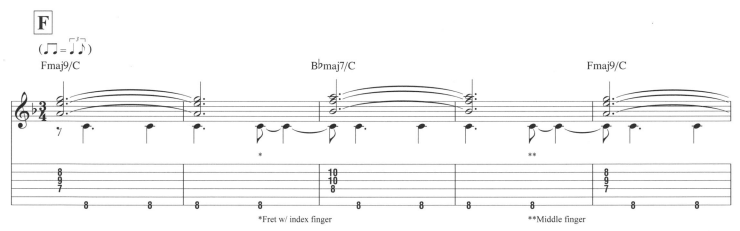

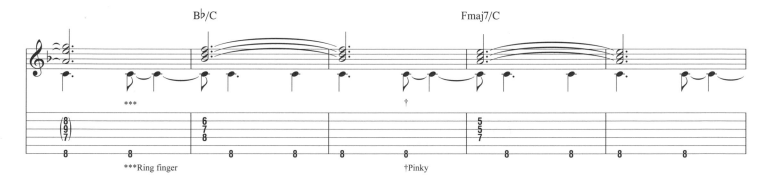

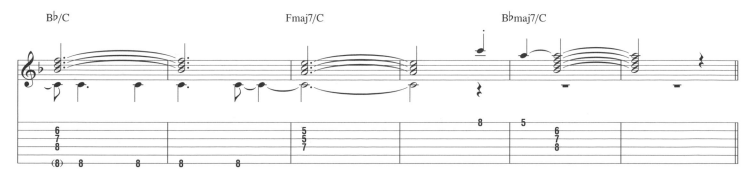

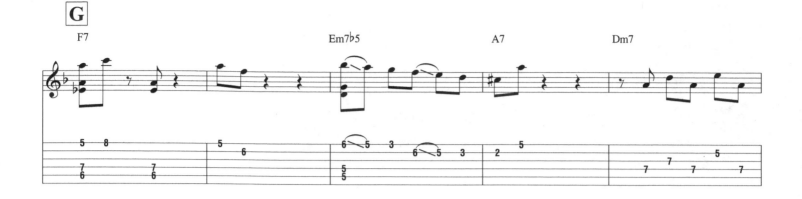

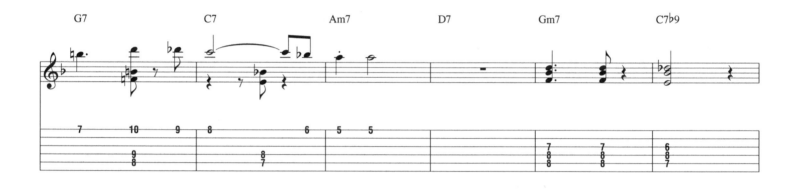

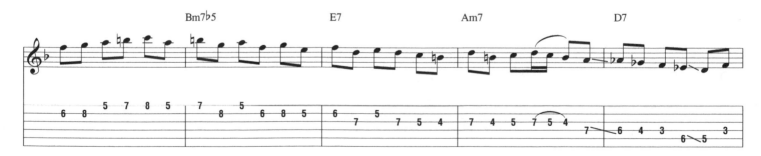

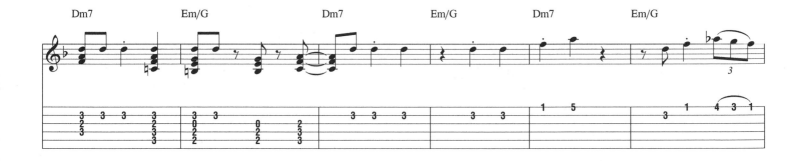

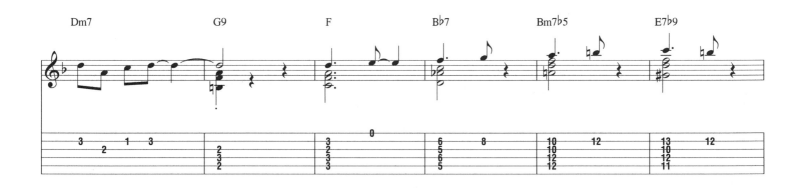

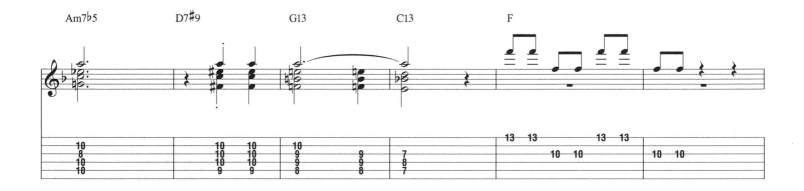

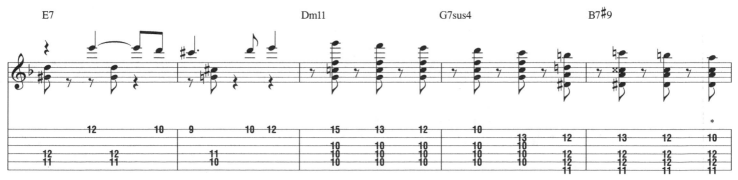

*Fret 2nd string w/ lower part of index finger.

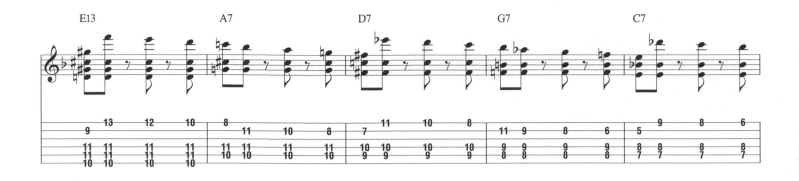

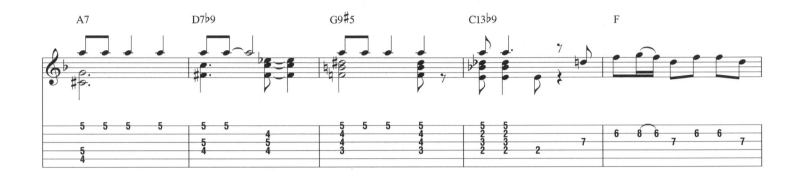

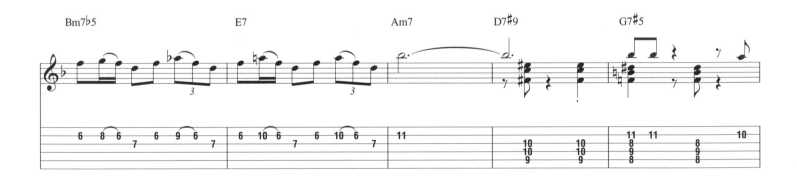

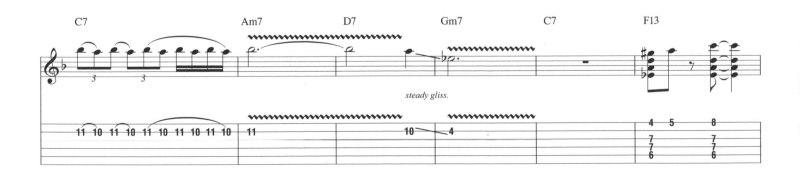

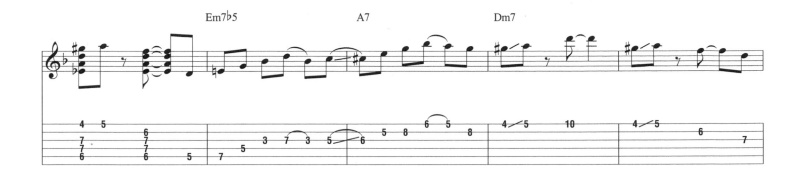

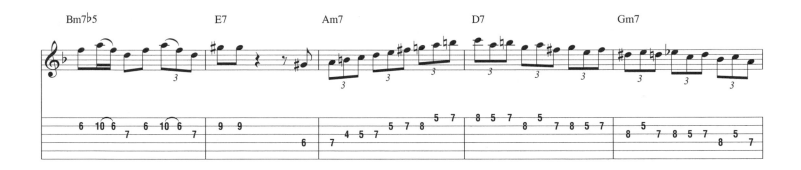

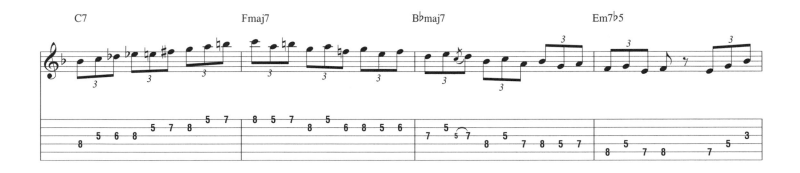

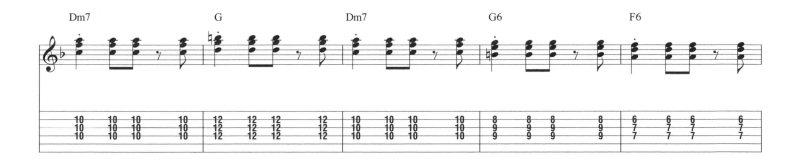

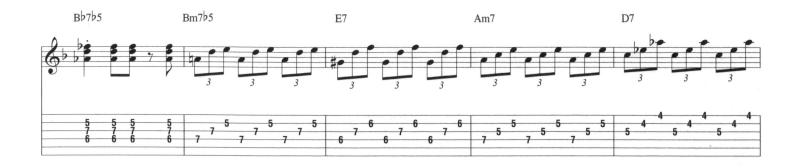

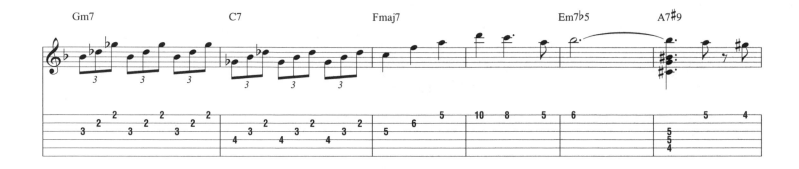

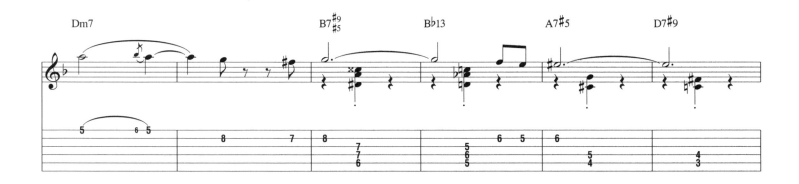

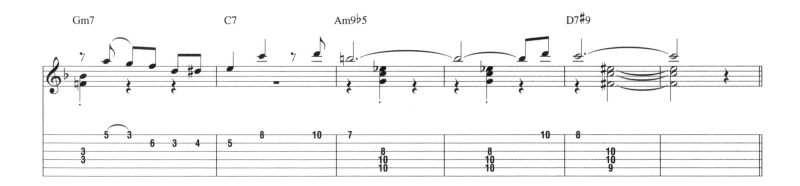

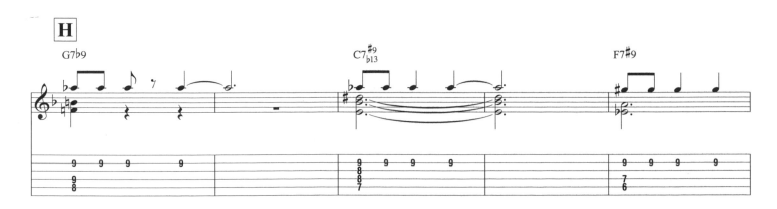

*Barre lowest 3 strings at 5th fret w/ middle finger.

**Fret lowest 2 strings at 5th fret w/ middle finger.

***Barre lowest 3 strings at 3rd fret w/ middle finger.

from *The Hallmark Sessions*

It Could Happen to You

from the Paramount Picture AND THE ANGELS SING

Words by Johnny Burke
Music by James Van Heusen

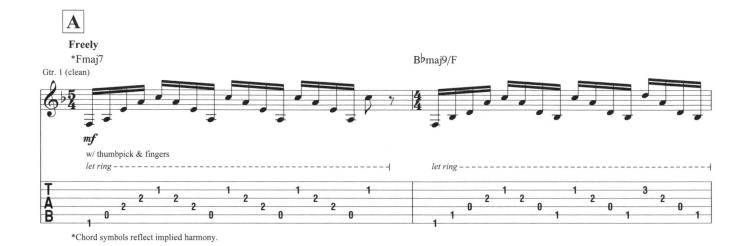

*Chord symbols reflect implied harmony.

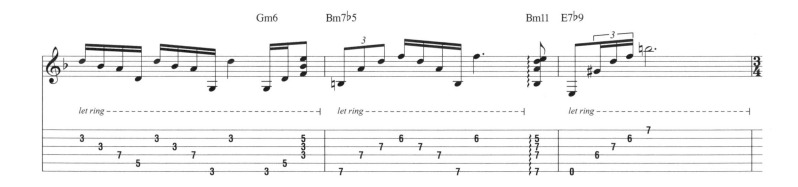

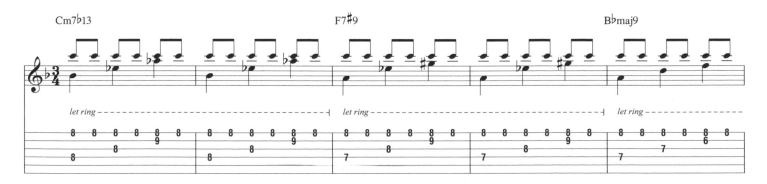

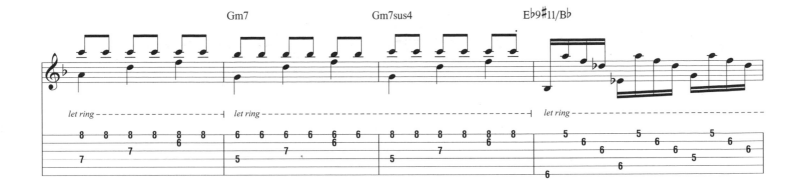

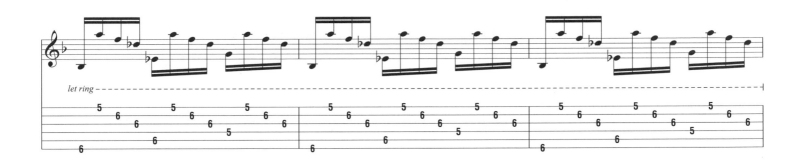

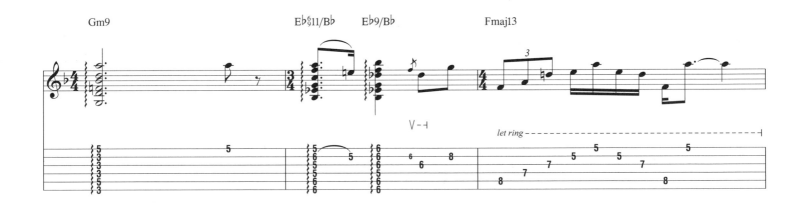

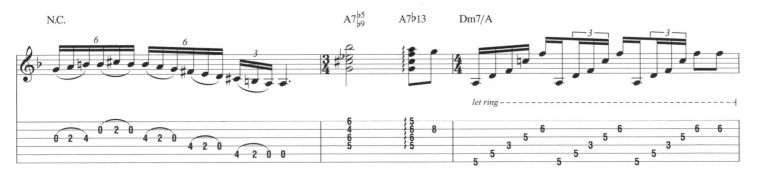

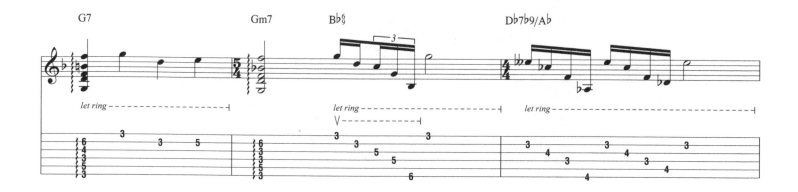

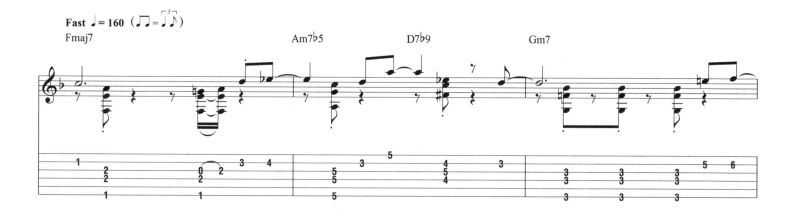

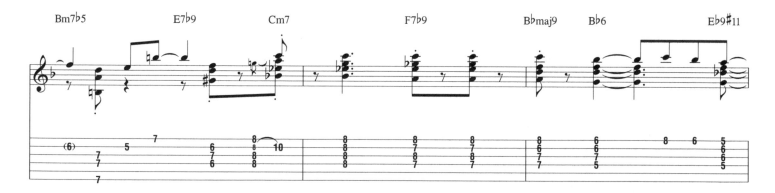

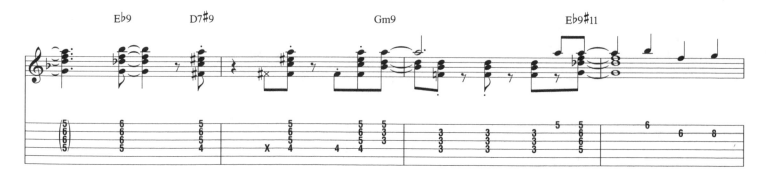

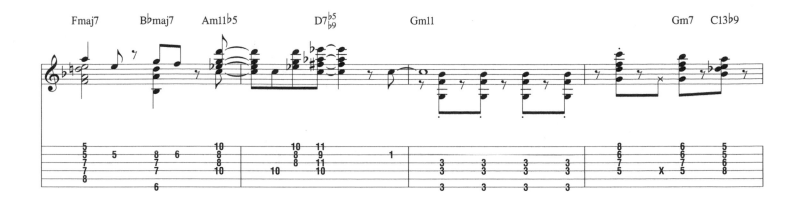

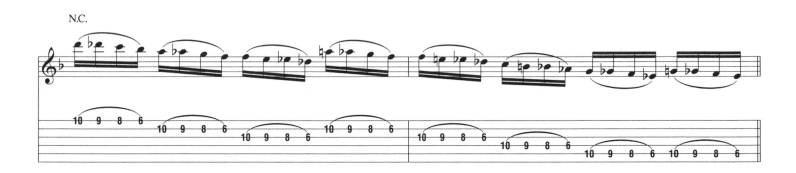

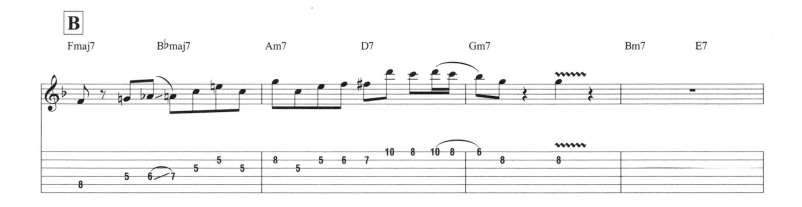

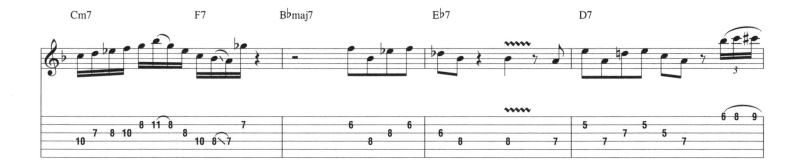

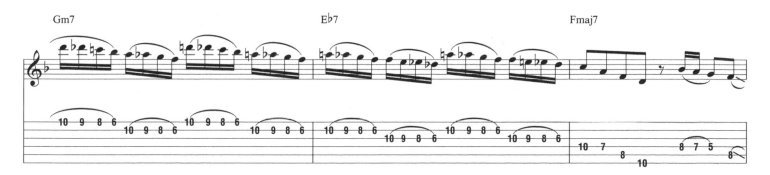

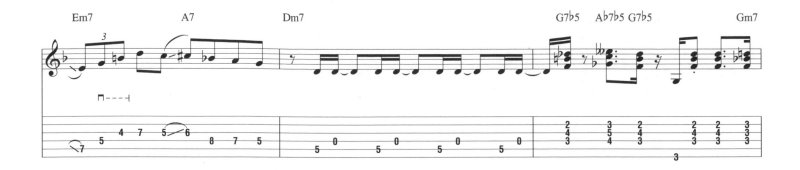

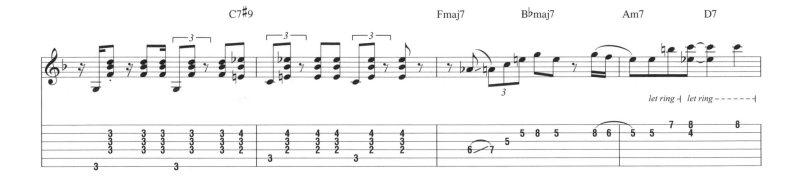

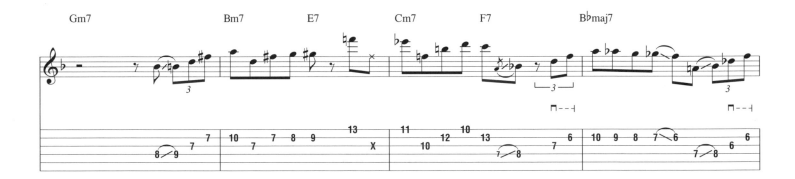

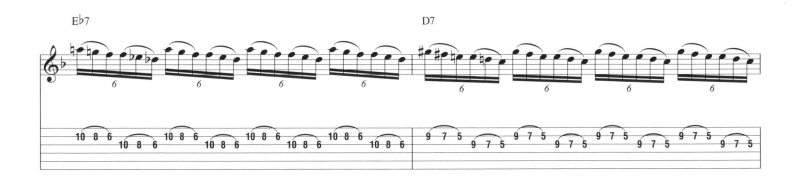

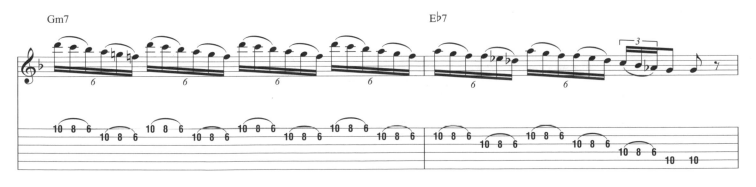

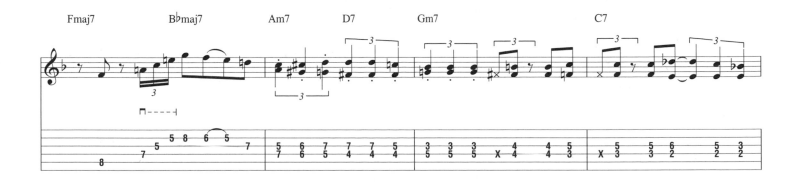

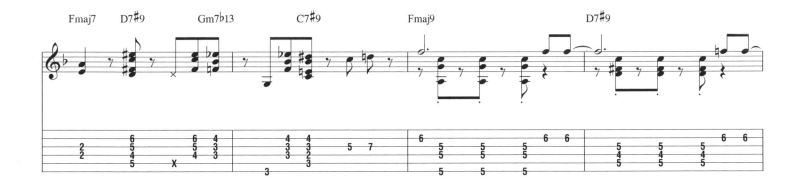

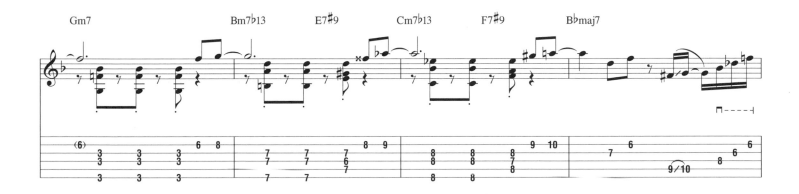

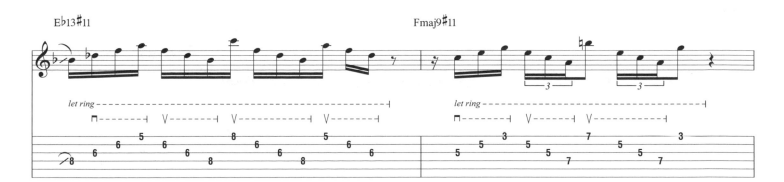

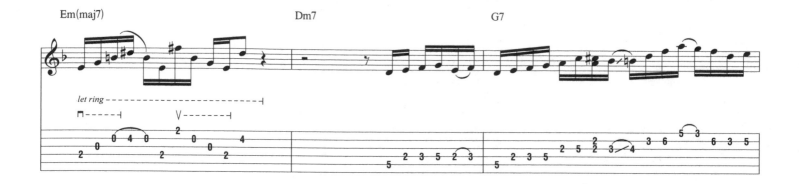

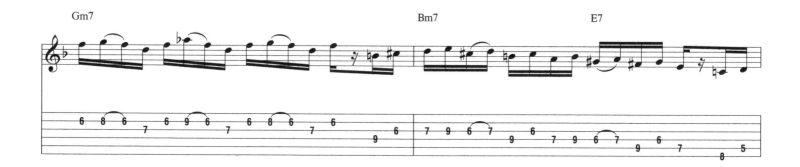

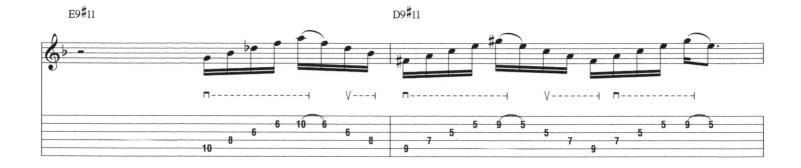

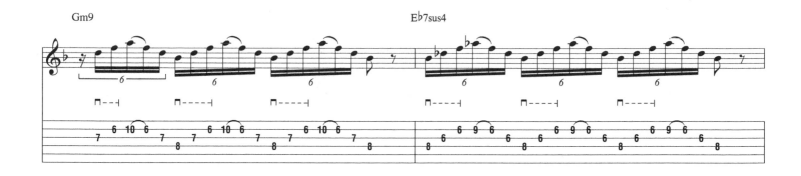

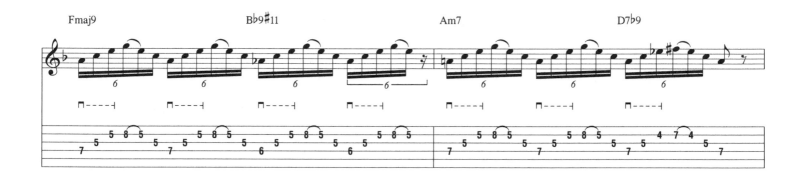

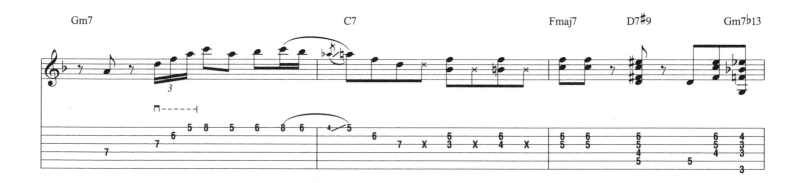

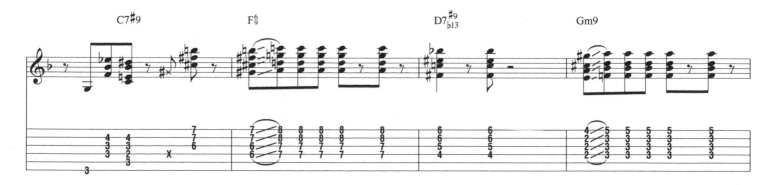

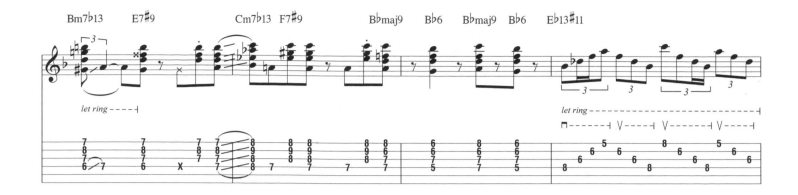

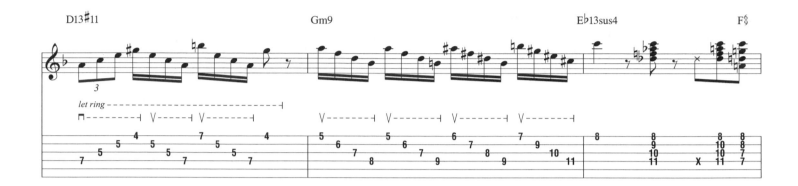

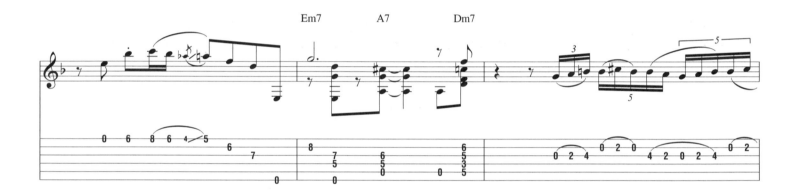

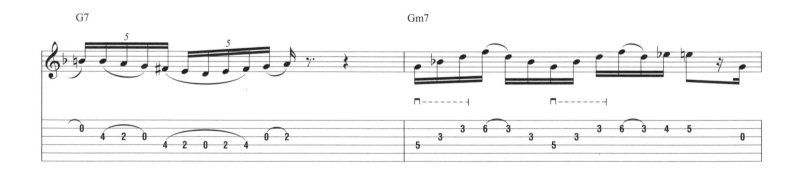

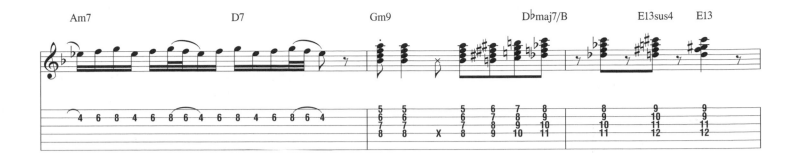

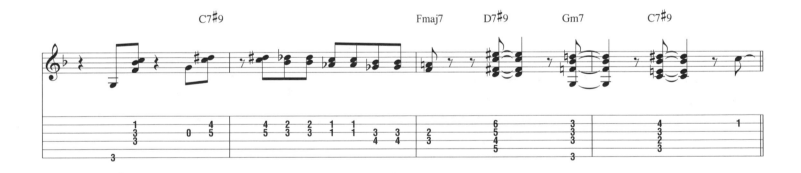

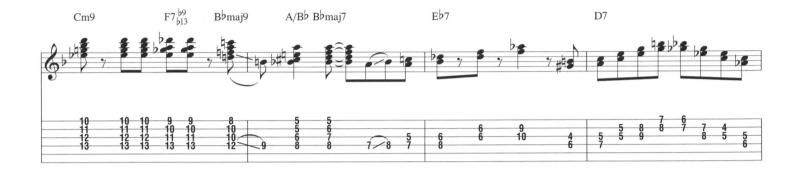

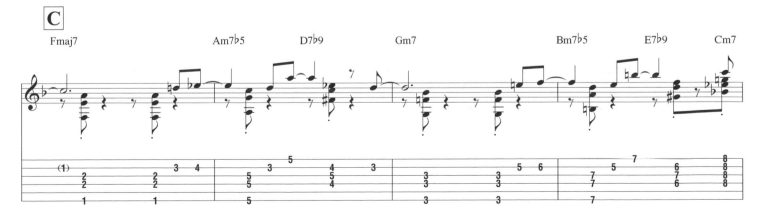

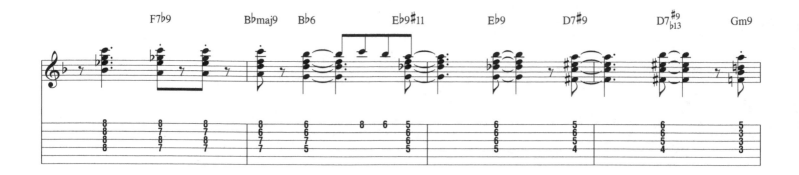

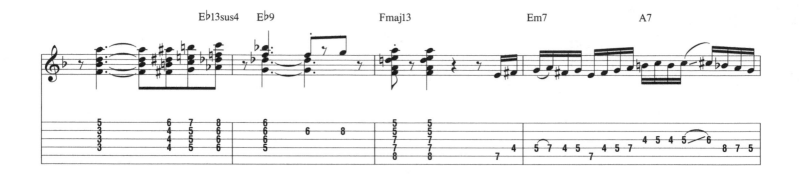

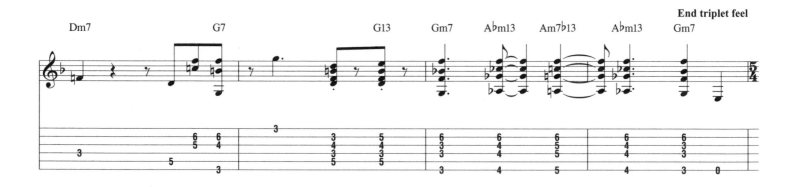

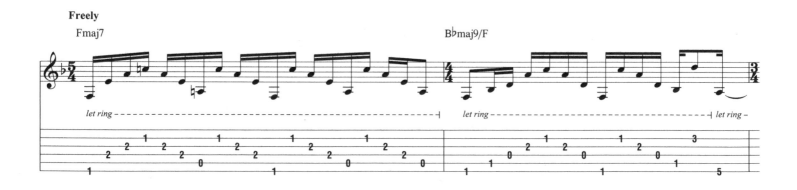

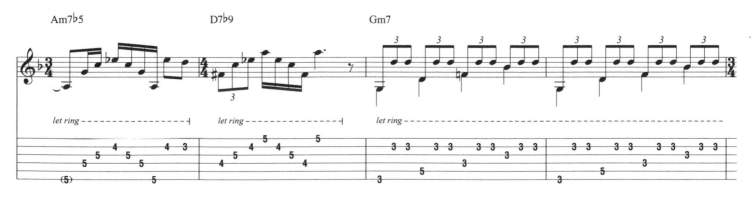

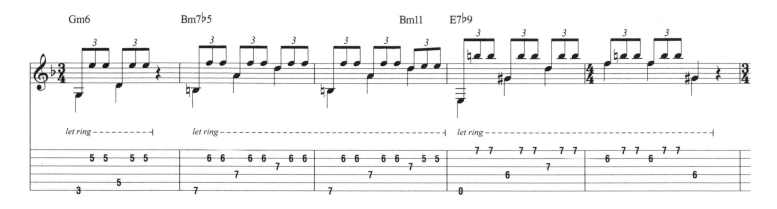

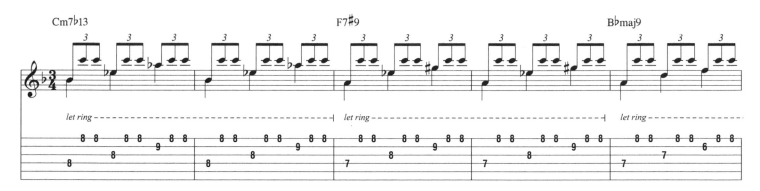

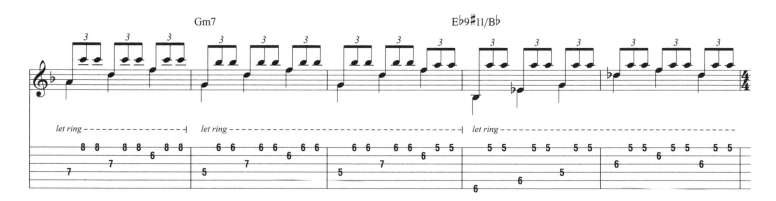

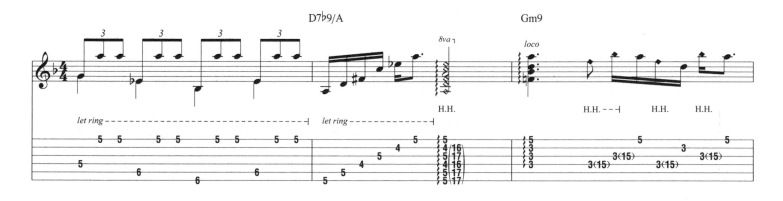

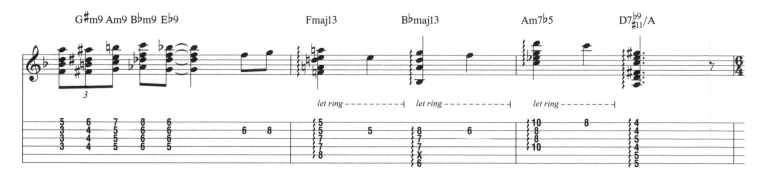

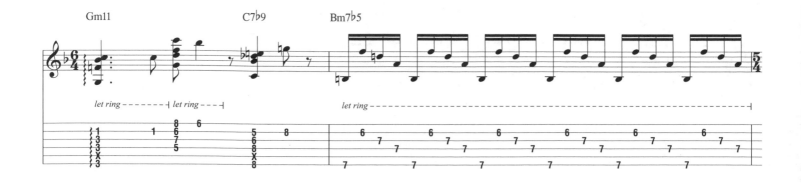

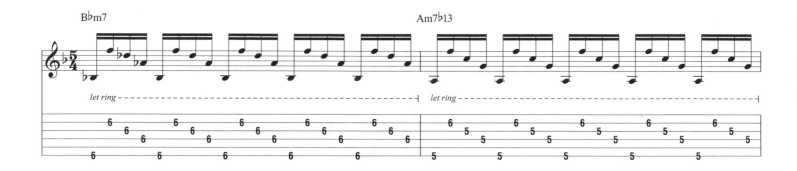

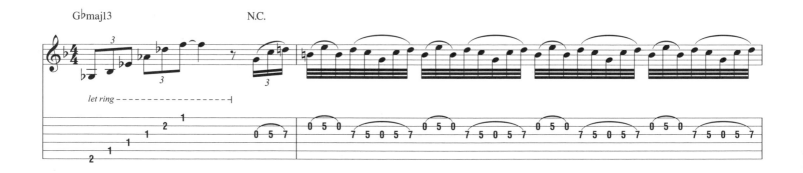

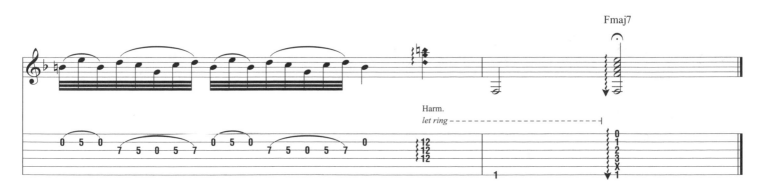

Oscar's Blues

By Oscar Moore

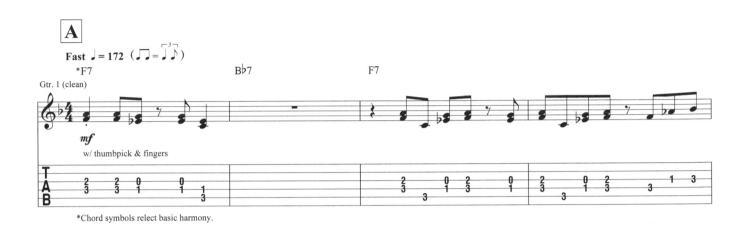

*Chord symbols relect basic harmony.

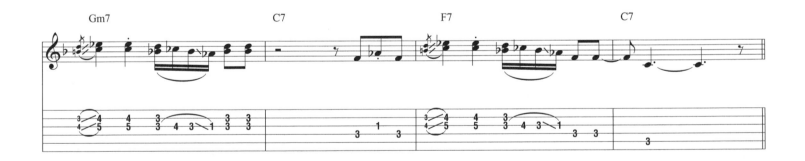

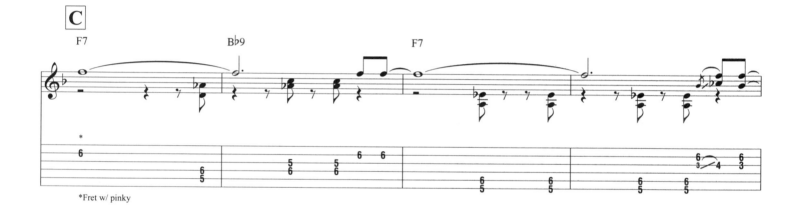

*Fret w/ pinky

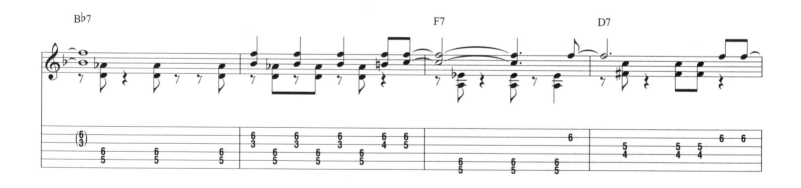

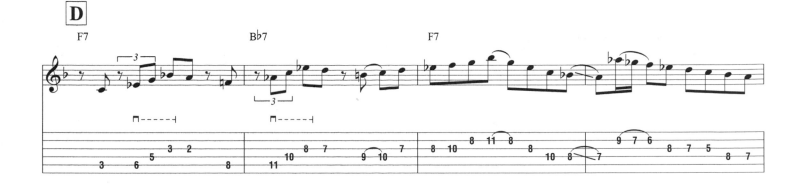

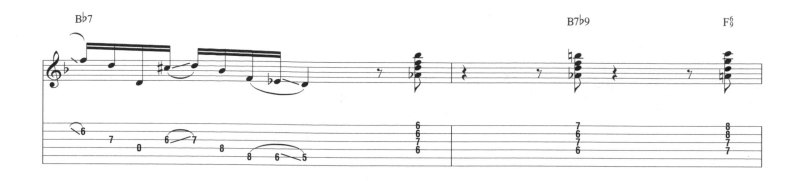

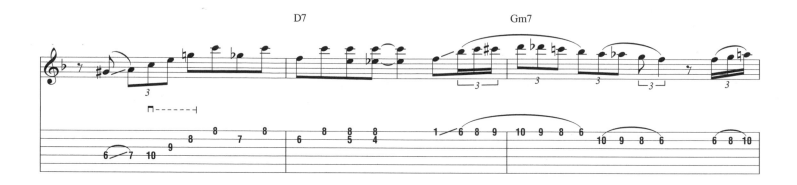

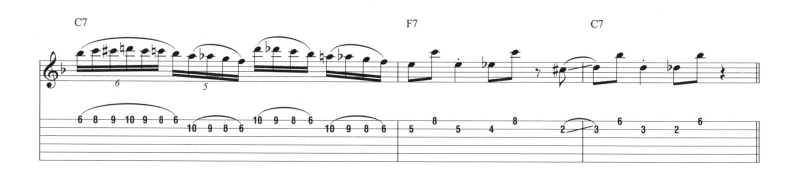

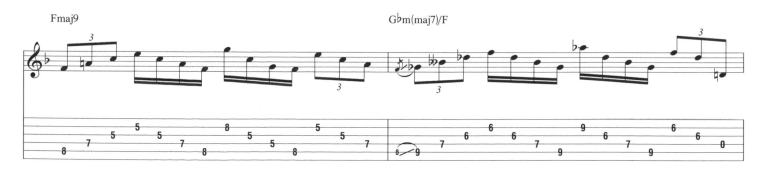

*Chord symbols reflect overall harmony.

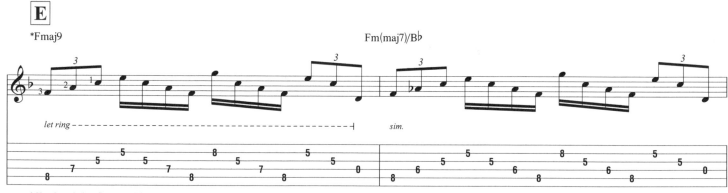

70

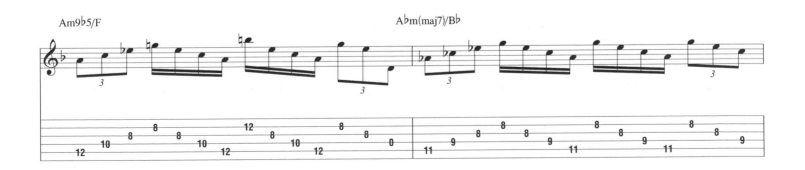

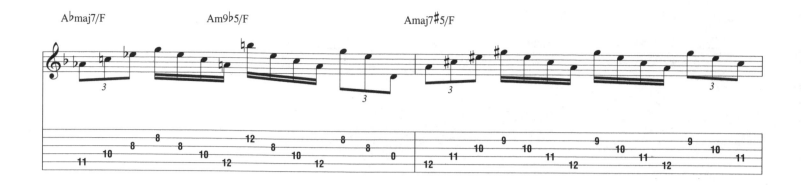

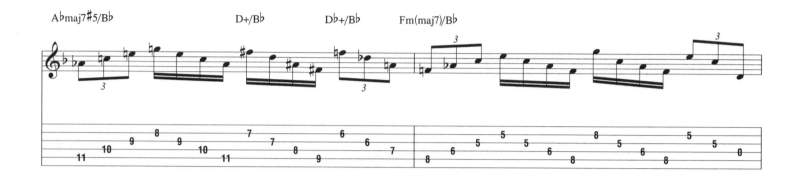

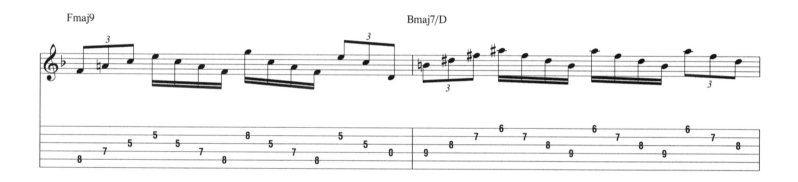

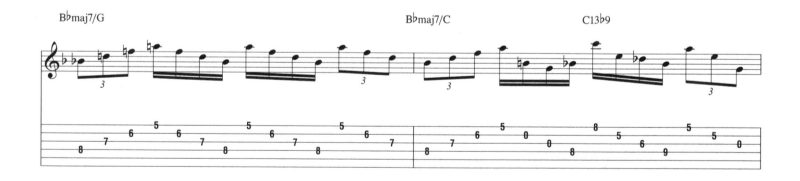

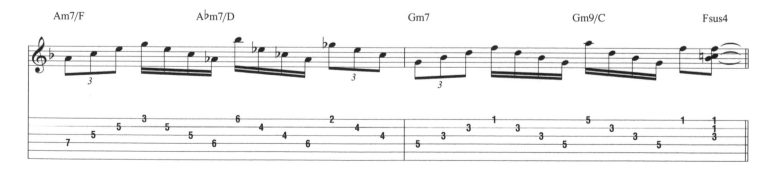

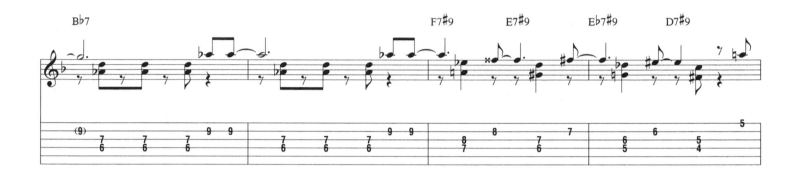

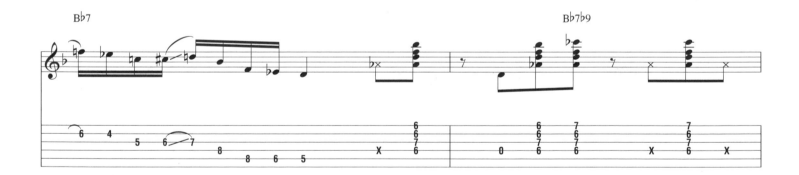

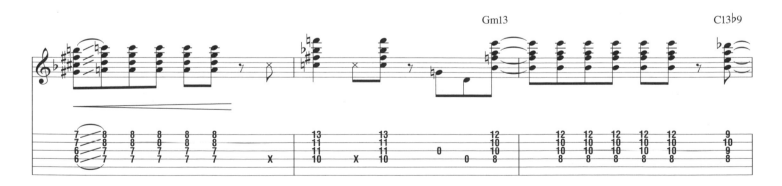

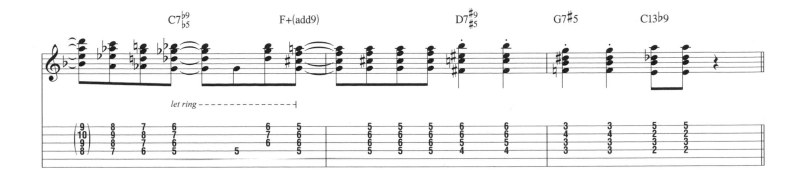

G

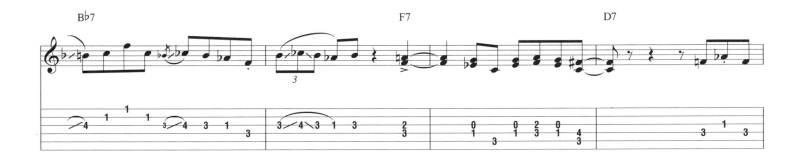

H

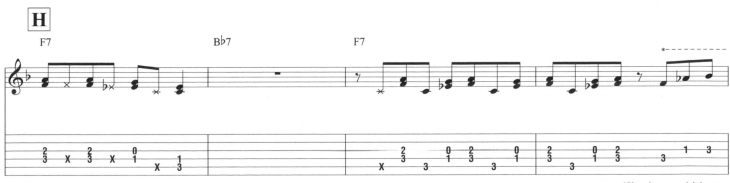

*Played as even eighth notes.

Spanjazz

By Lenny Breau

Capo II

*Symbols in parentheses represent chord names respective to capoed guitar.
Symbols above reflect actual sounding chords. Capoed fret is "0" in tab.
Chord symbols reflect implied harmony.

**Tap on face of guitar with right-
hand fingers in specified rhythm.

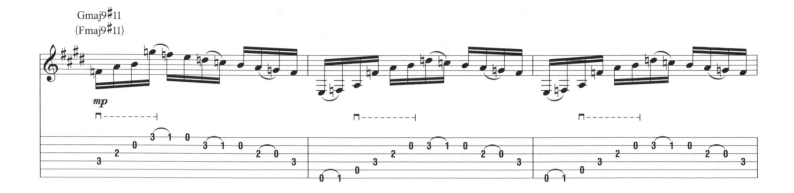

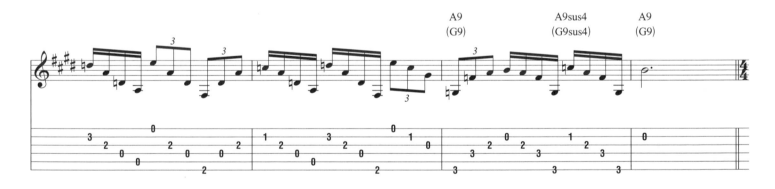

B

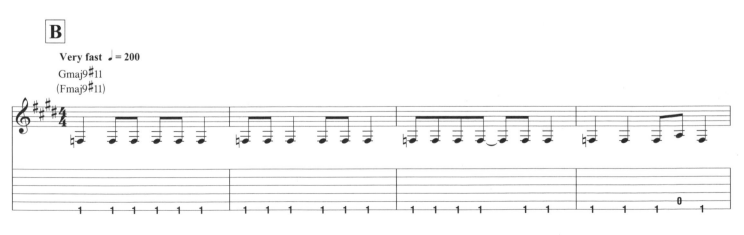

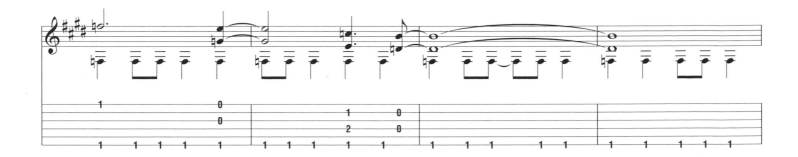

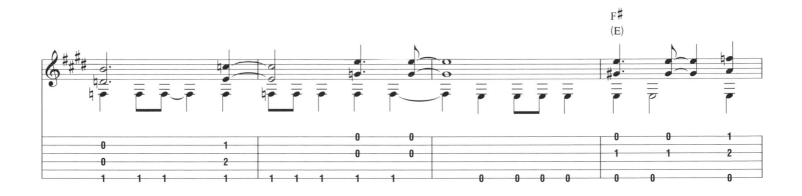

F#
(E)

*P.M. - - - - -

*P.M. above staff refers
to upstemmed notes only.

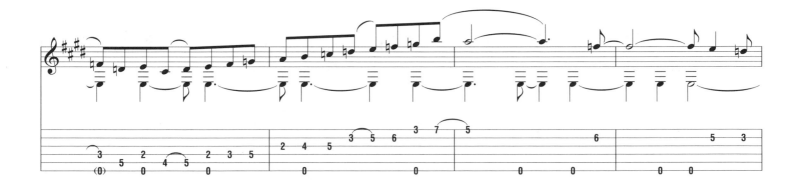

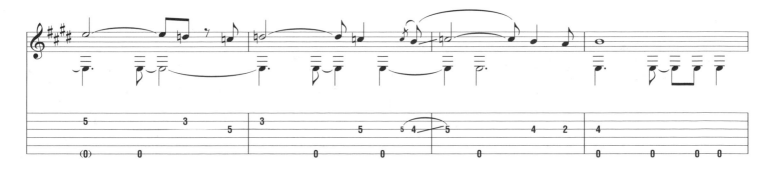

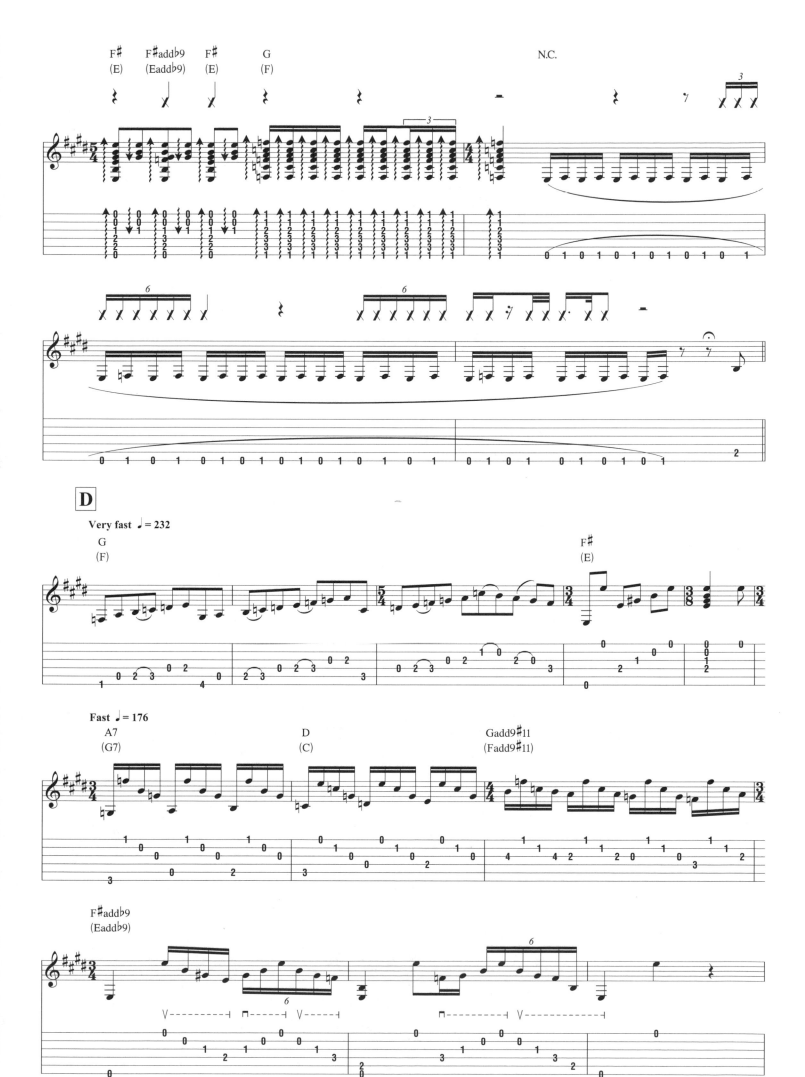

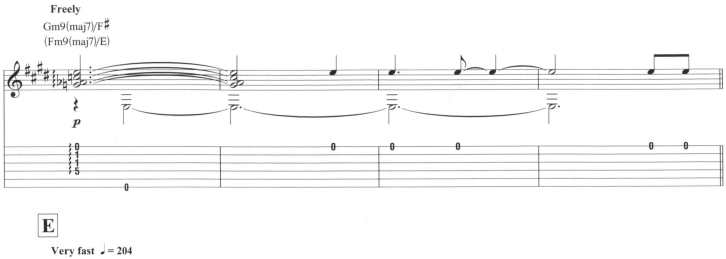

Freely

E

Very fast ♩ = 204

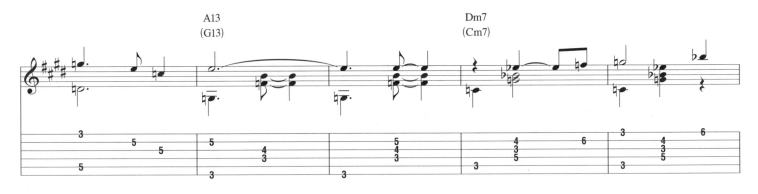

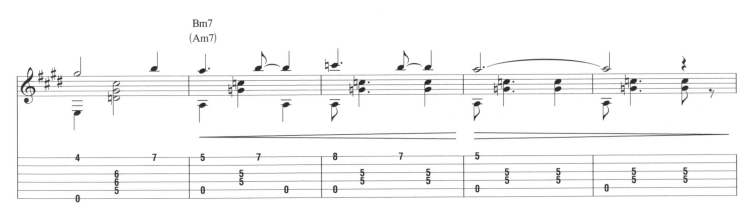

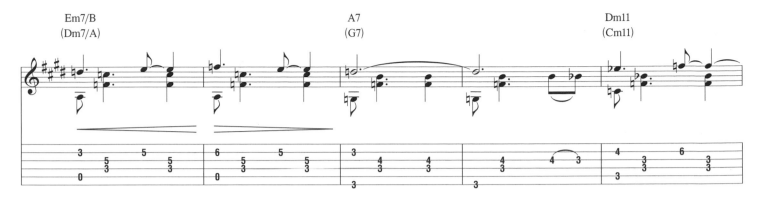

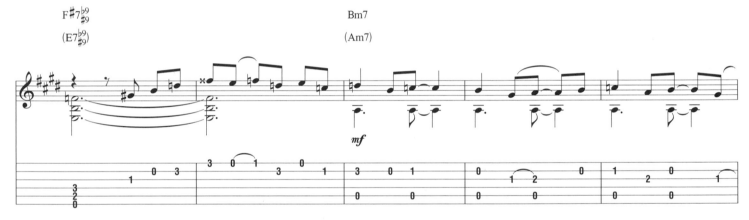

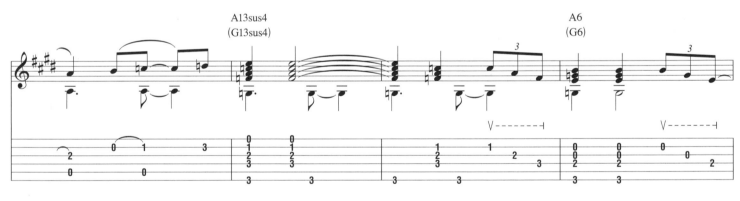

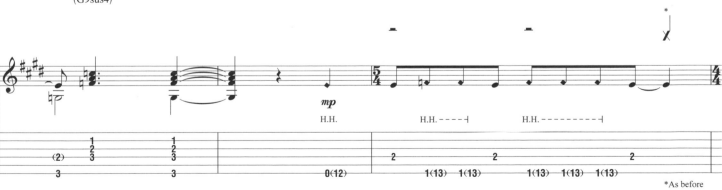

*As before

Gmaj13
(Fmaj13)

F#7
(E7)

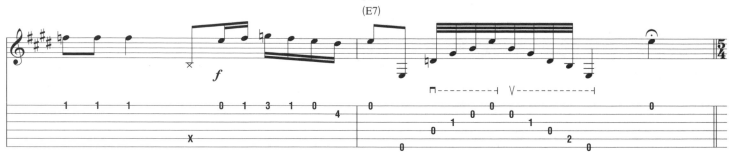

F

Fast ♩ = 160

F#7
(E7)

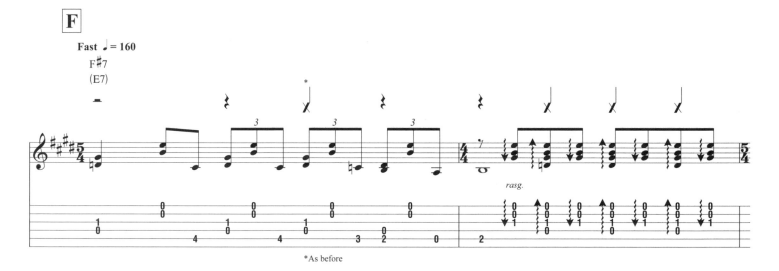

*As before

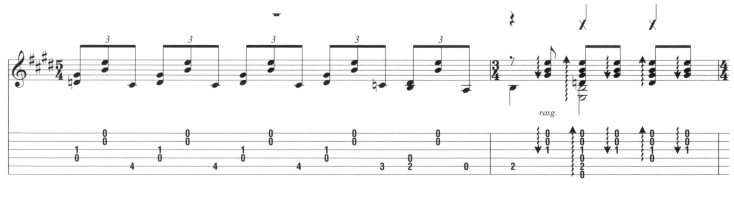

F#7♭9
(E7♭9)

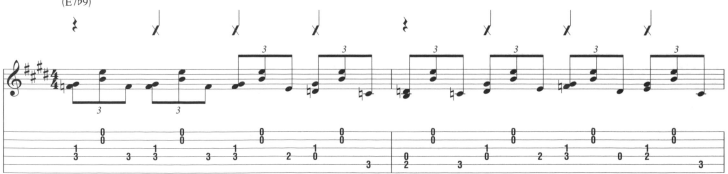

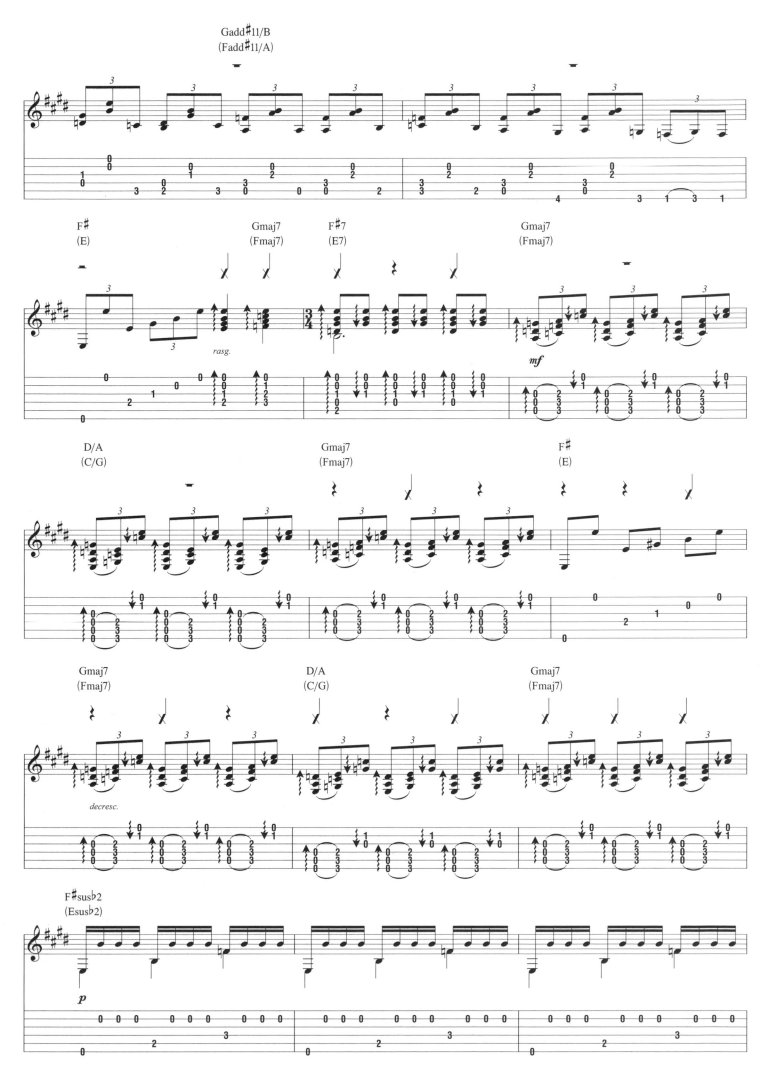

F#5
(E5)

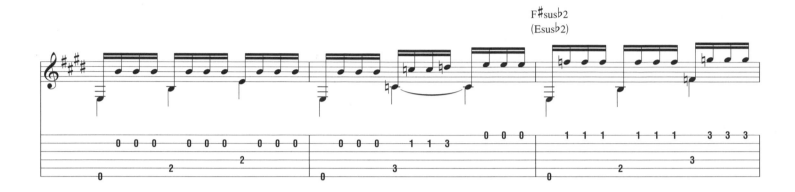

F#sus♭2
(Esus♭2)

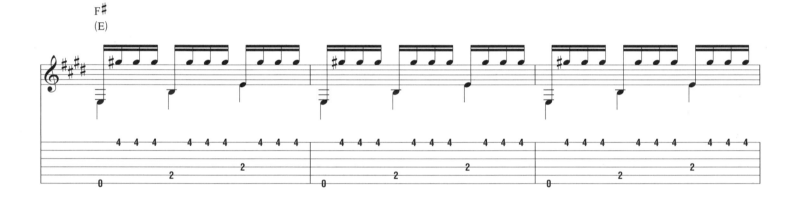

F#
(E)

F#5
(E5)

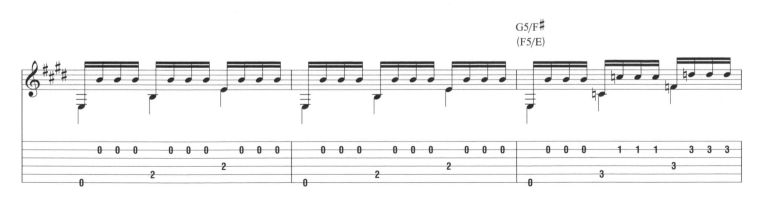

G5/F#
(F5/E)

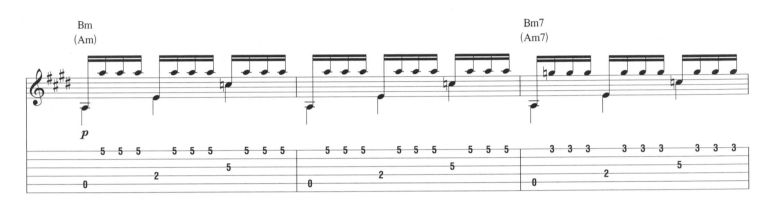

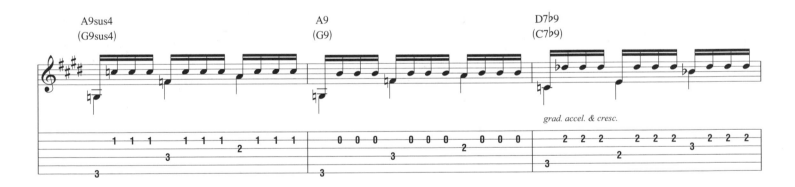

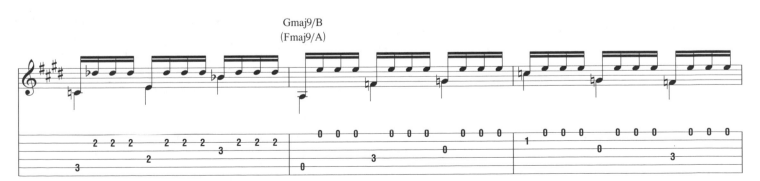

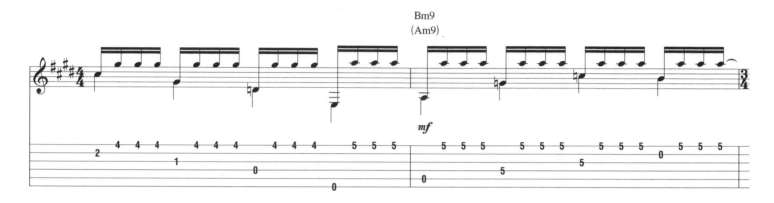

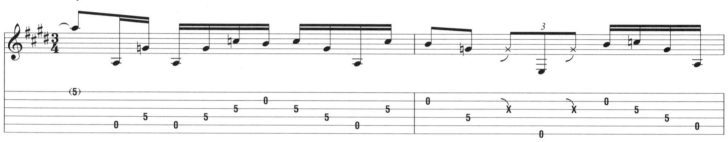

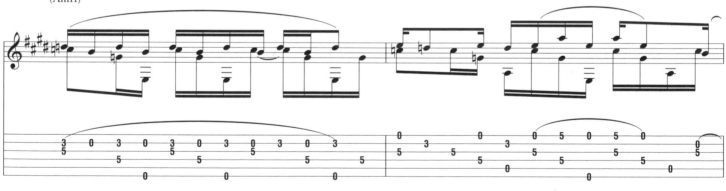

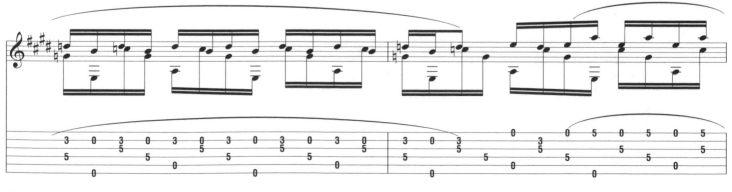

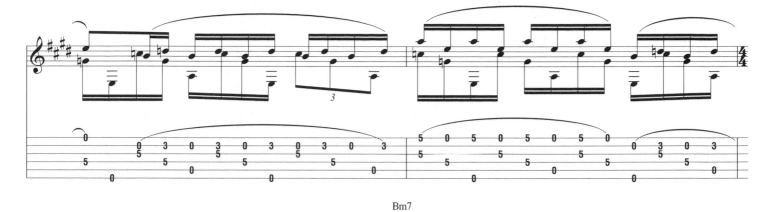

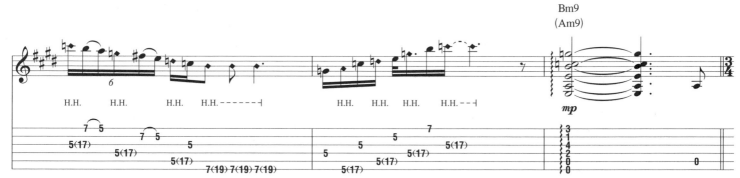

G

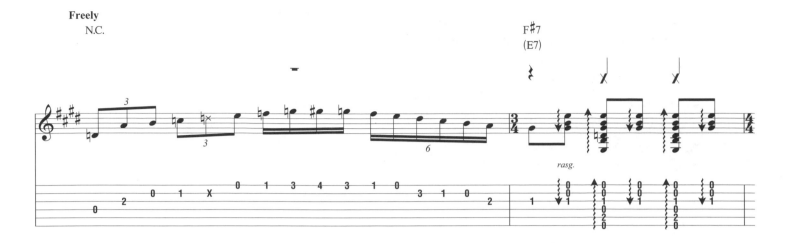

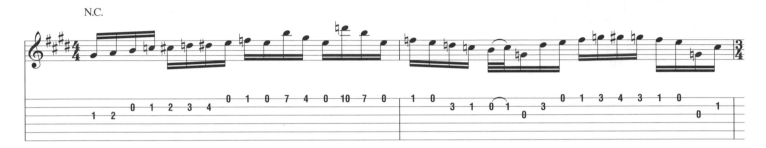

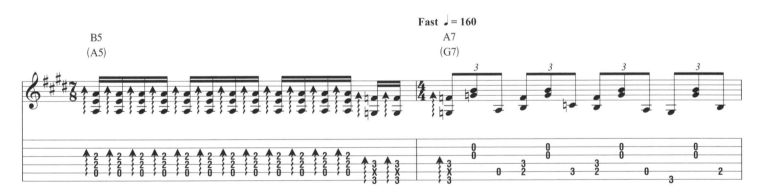

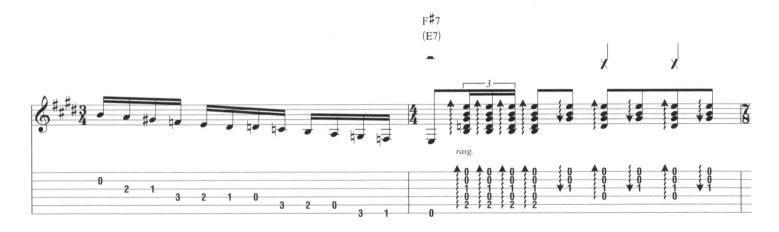

*sul ponticello (pick near bridge).

Taranta

By Lenny Breau

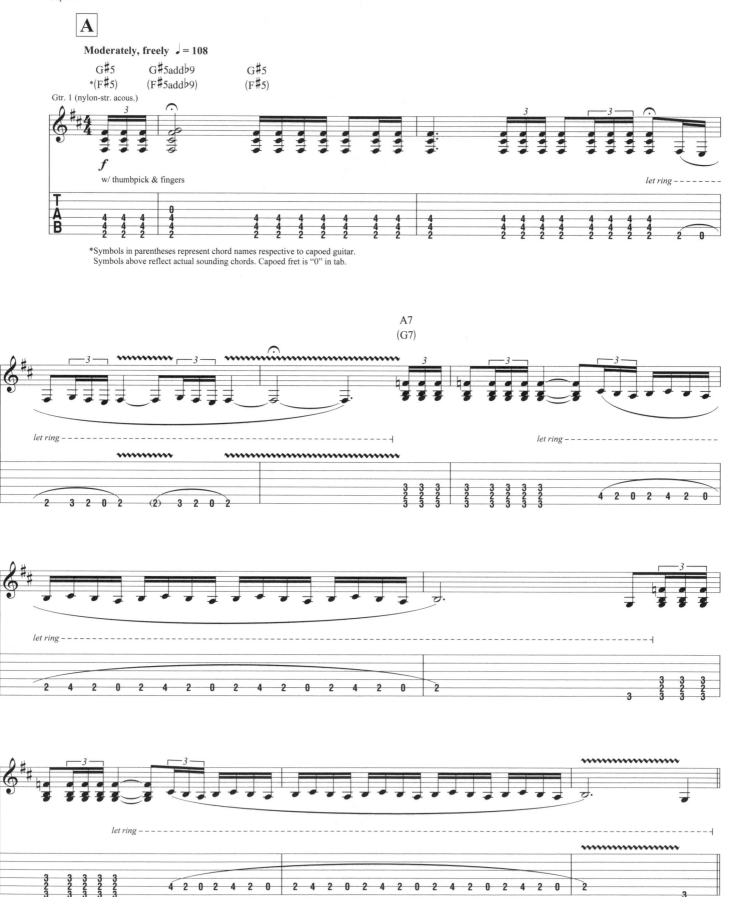

*Symbols in parentheses represent chord names respective to capoed guitar.
Symbols above reflect actual sounding chords. Capoed fret is "0" in tab.

N.C.

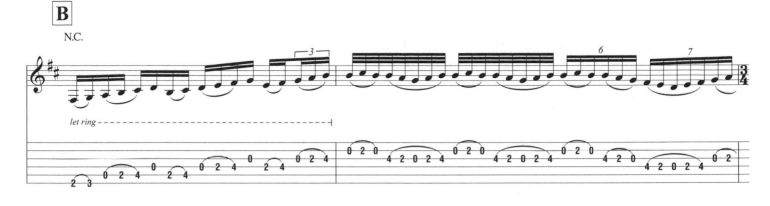

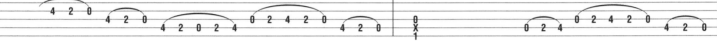

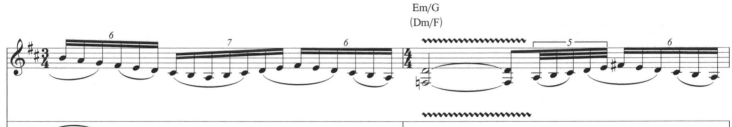

Em/G
(Dm/F)

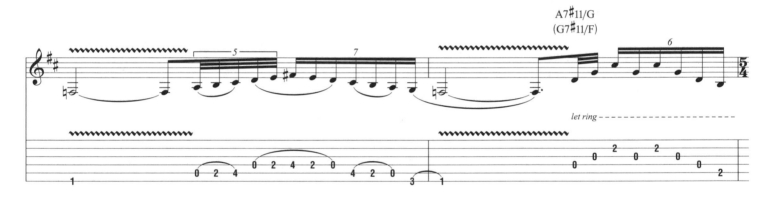

A7♯11/G
(G7♯11/F)

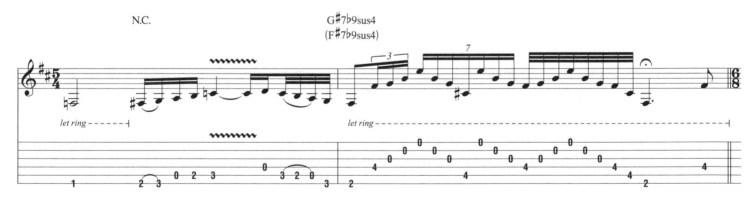

N.C.

G♯7♭9sus4
(F♯7♭9sus4)

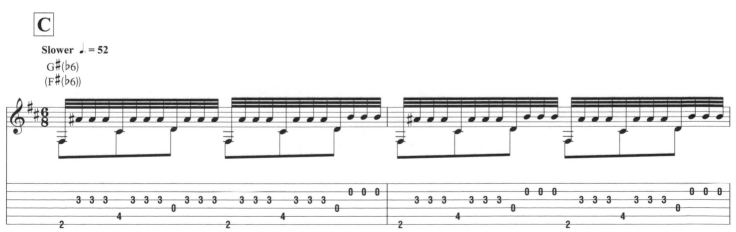

C

Slower ♩. = 52

G♯(♭6)
(F♯(♭6))

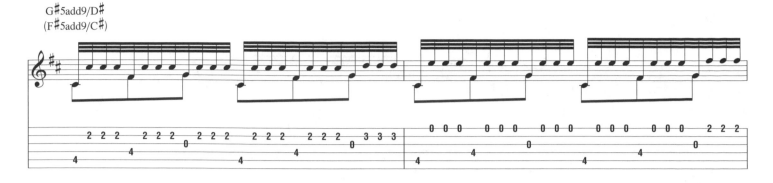

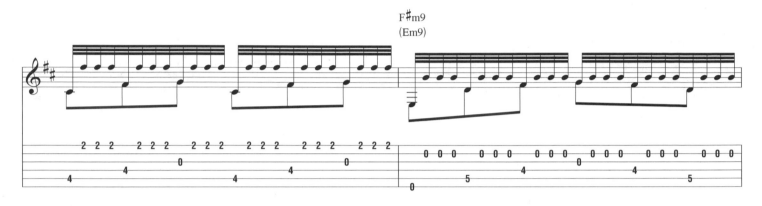

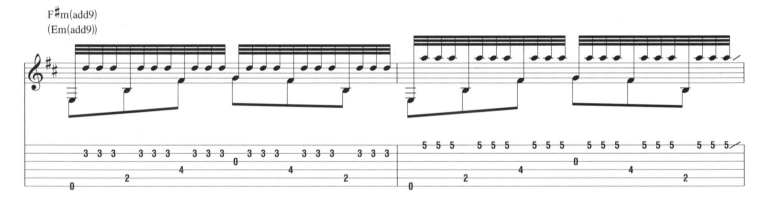

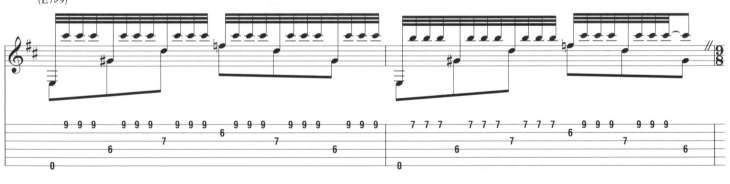

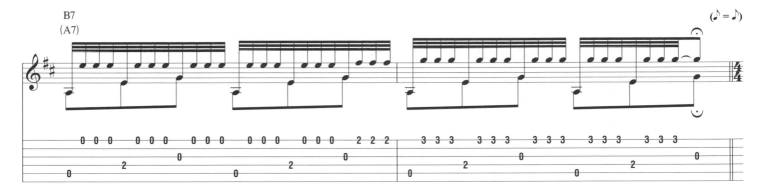

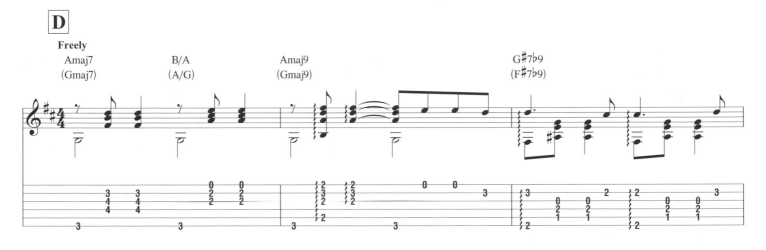

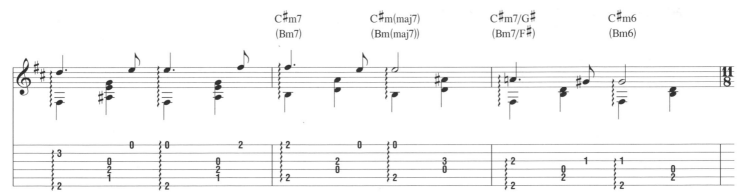

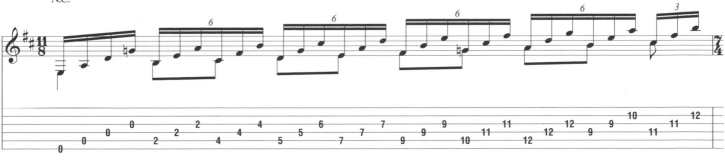

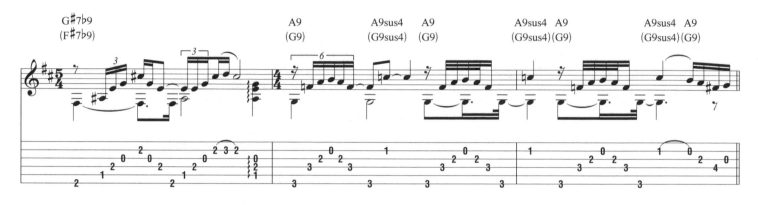

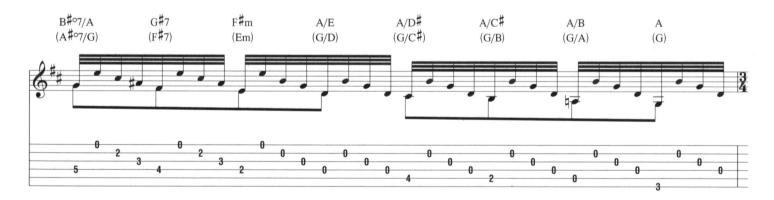

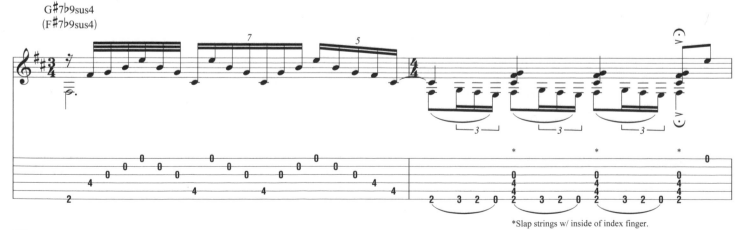

*Slap strings w/ inside of index finger.

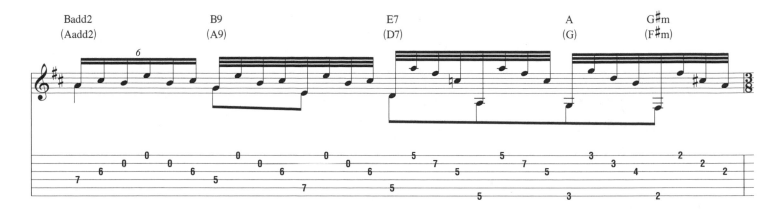

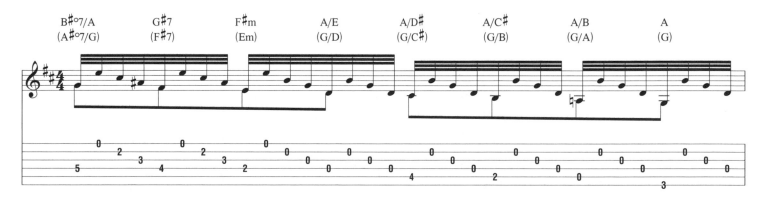

F

Faster ♩ = 152

F#m11
(Em11)

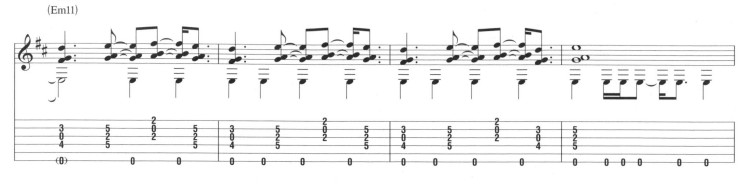

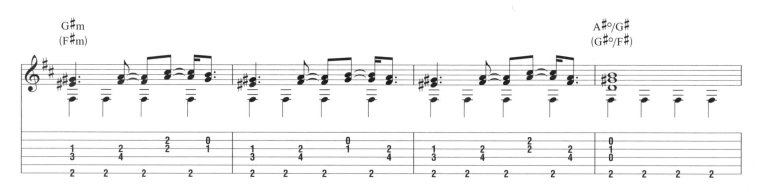

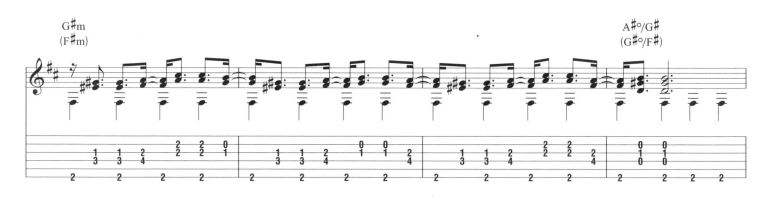

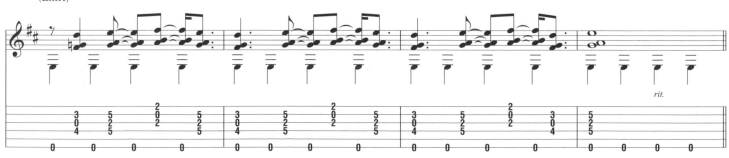

G

Slower ♩ = 140

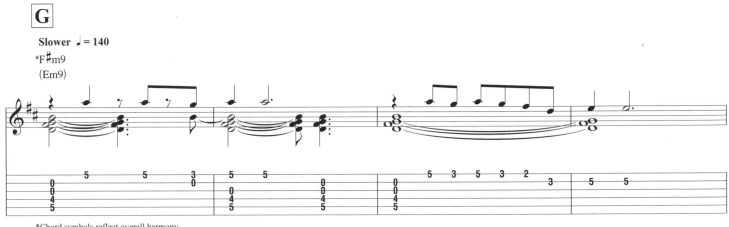

*Chord symbols reflect overall harmony.

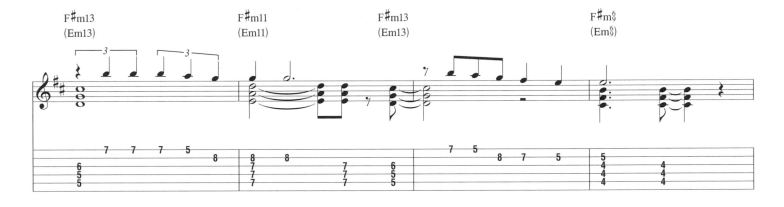

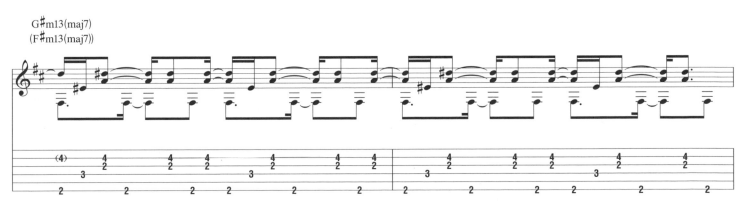

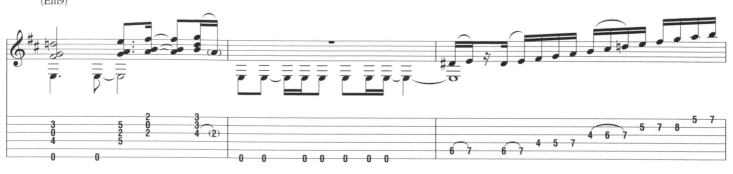

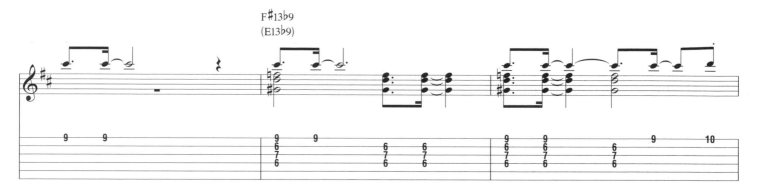

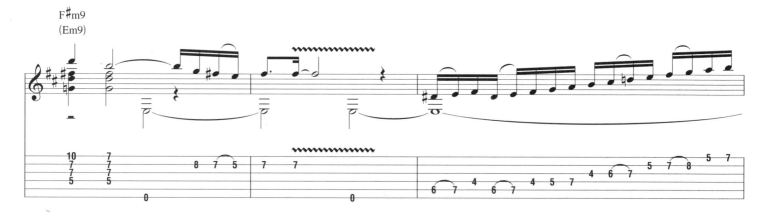

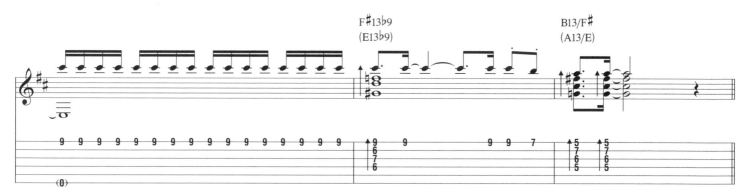

J

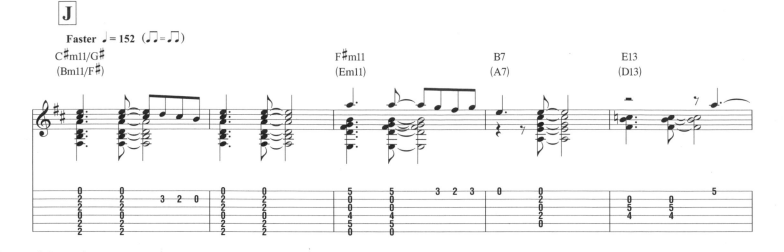

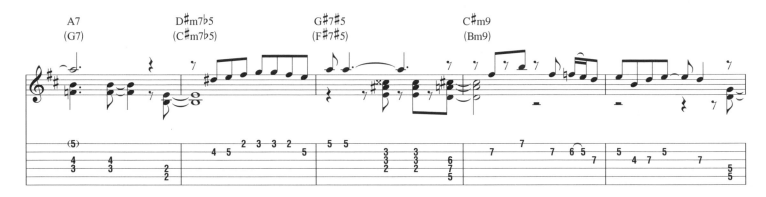

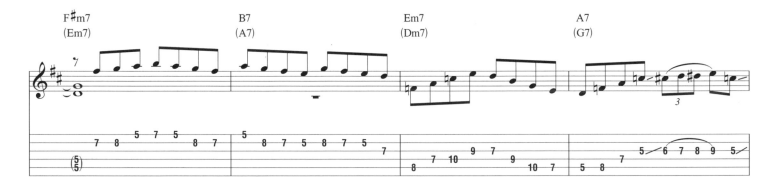

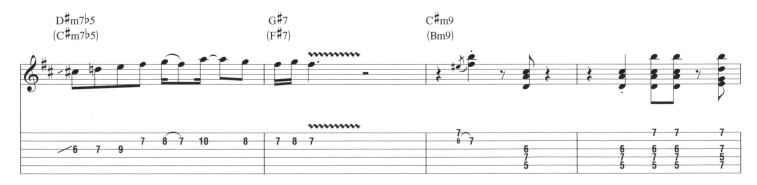

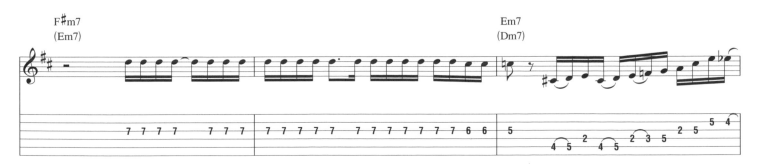

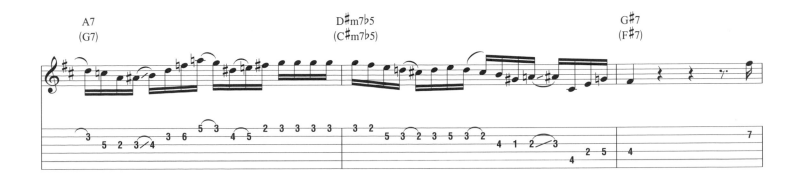

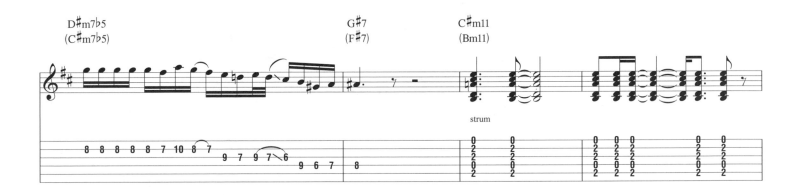

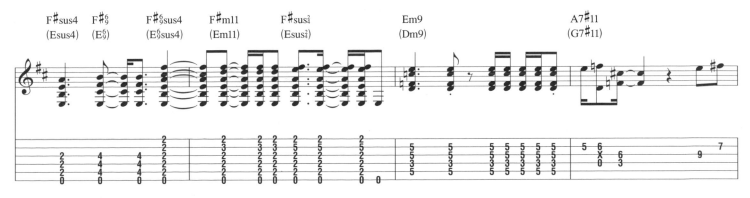

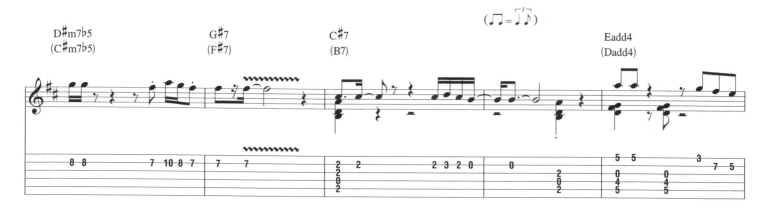

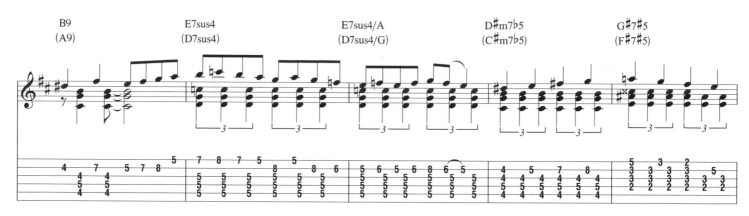

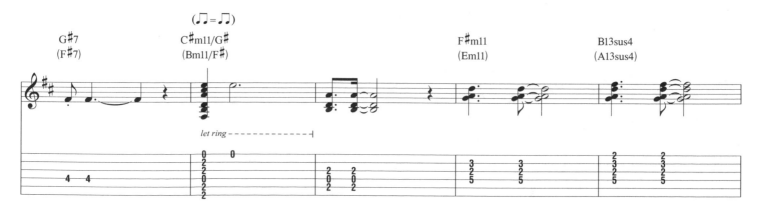

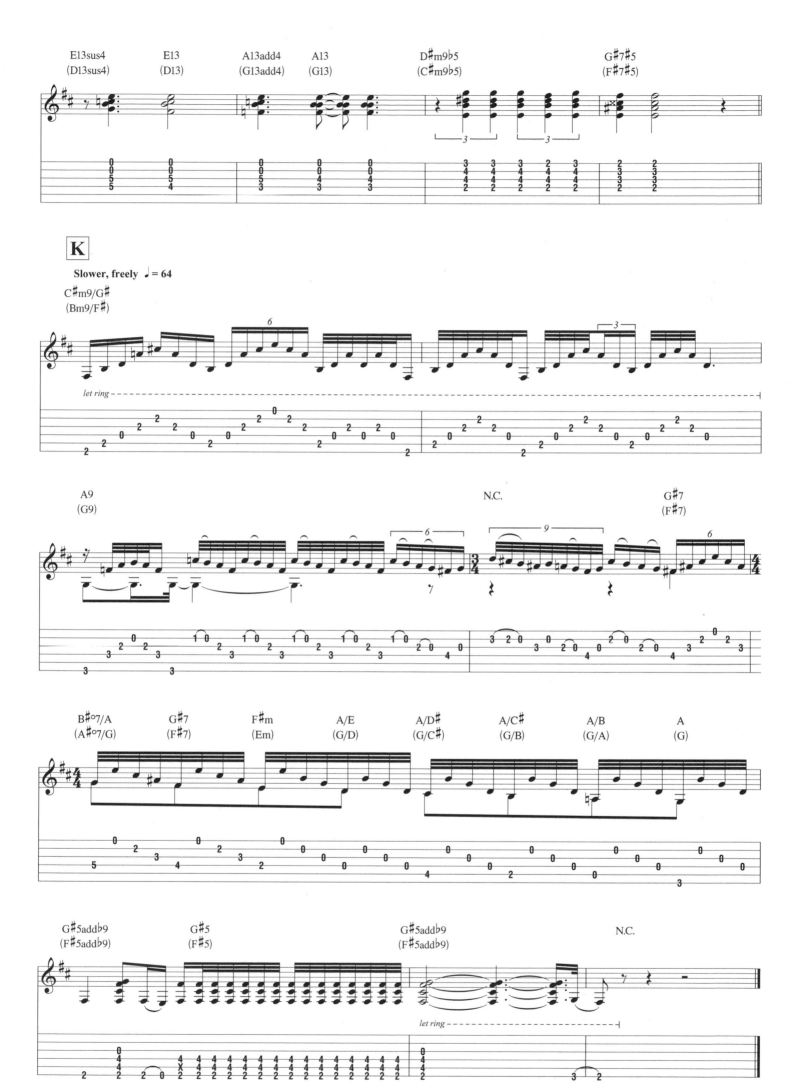

There Is No Greater Love

Words by Marty Symes
Music by Isham Jones

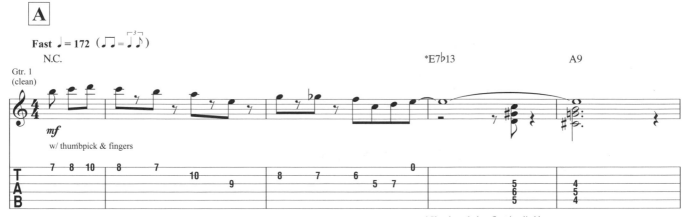

*Chord symbols reflect implied harmony.

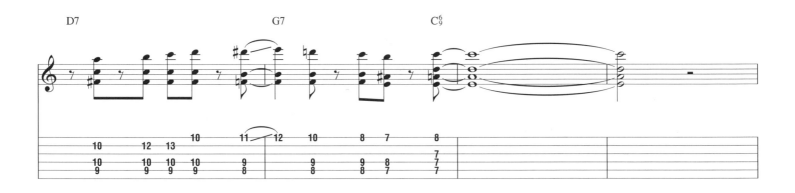

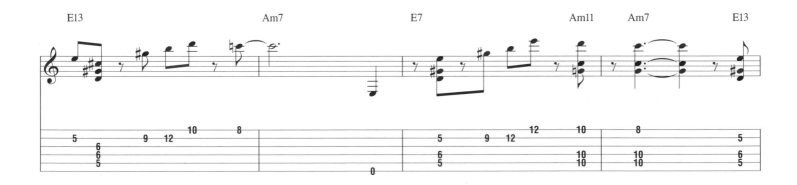

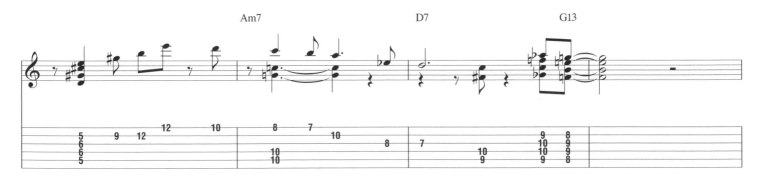

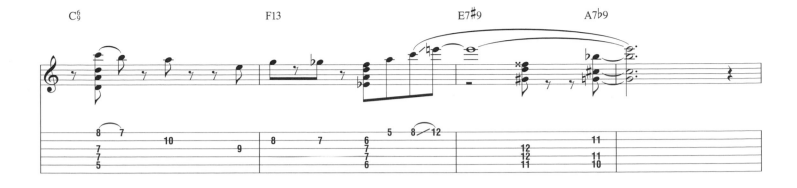

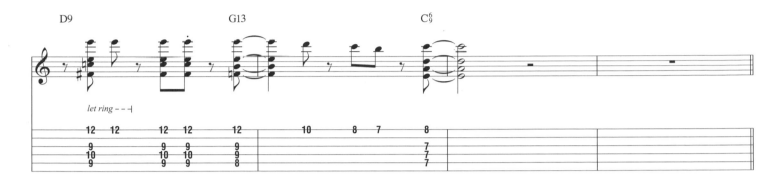

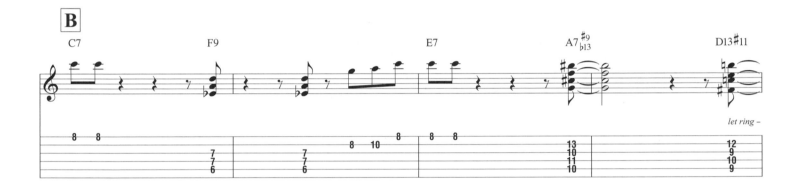

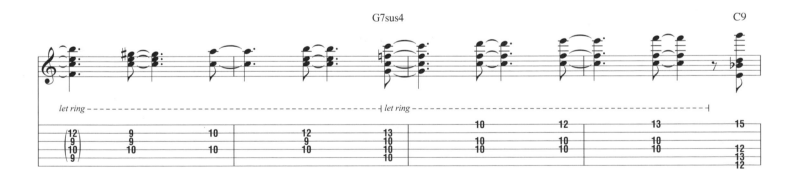

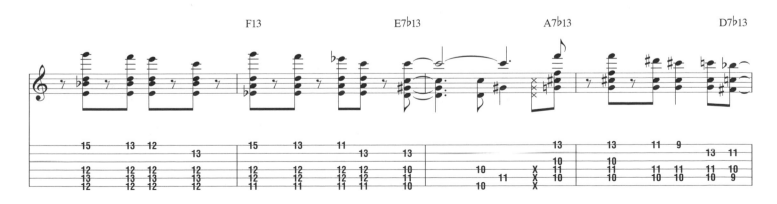

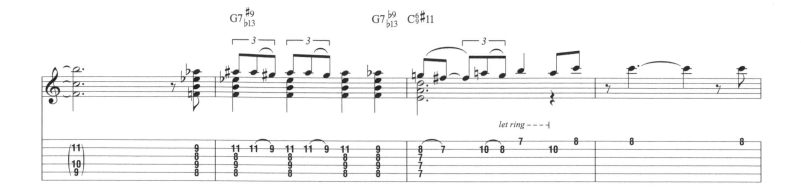

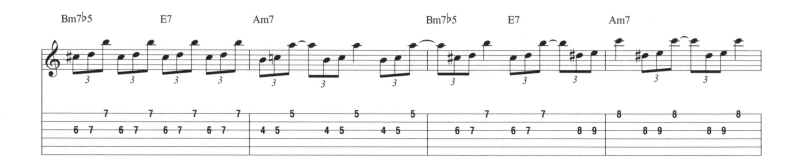

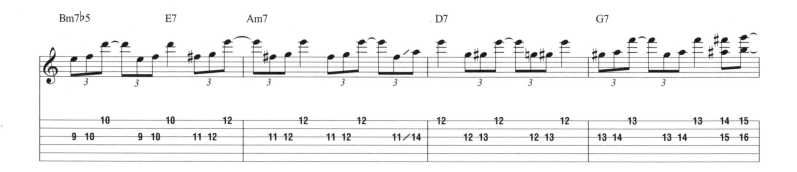

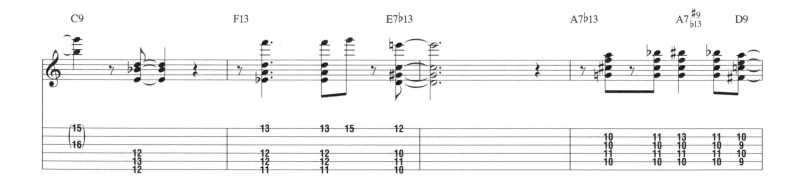

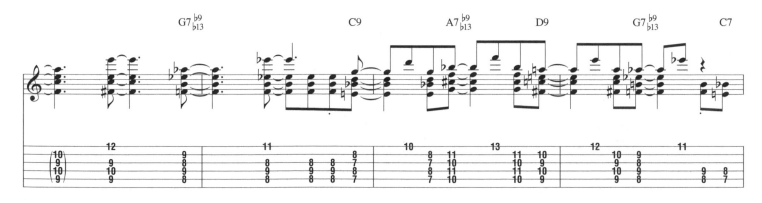

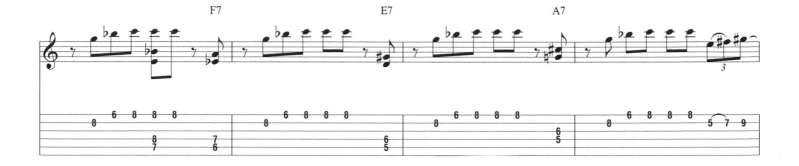

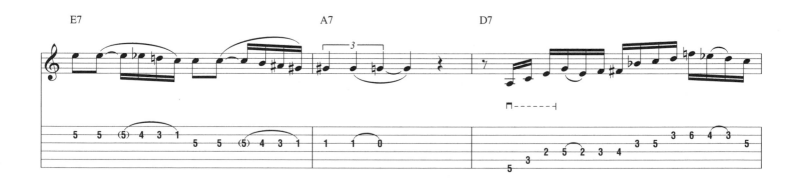

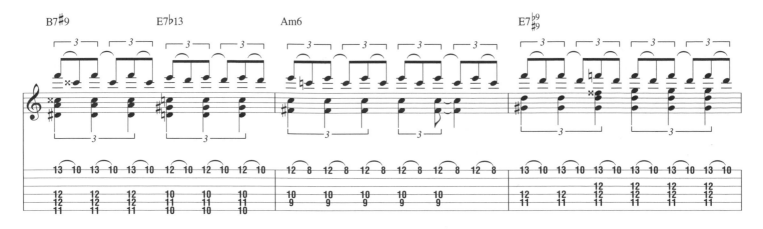

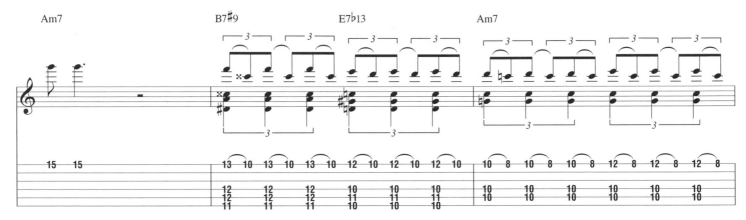

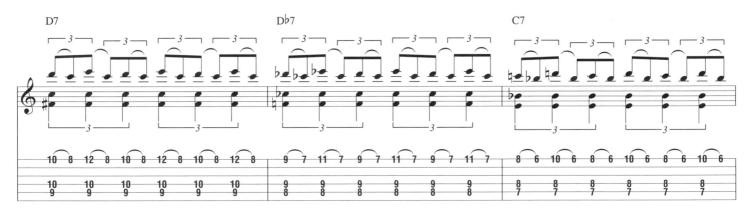

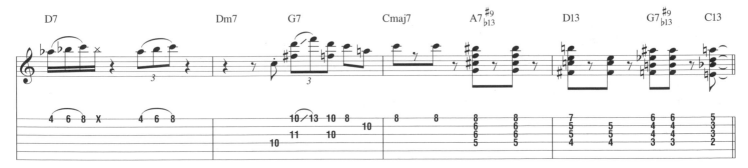

C

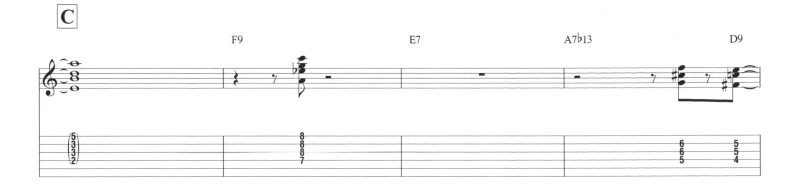

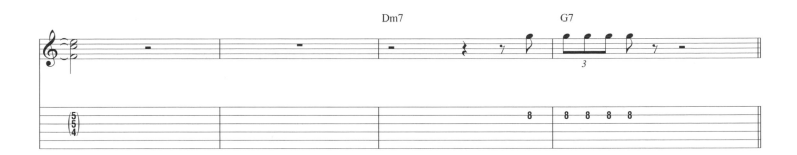

D

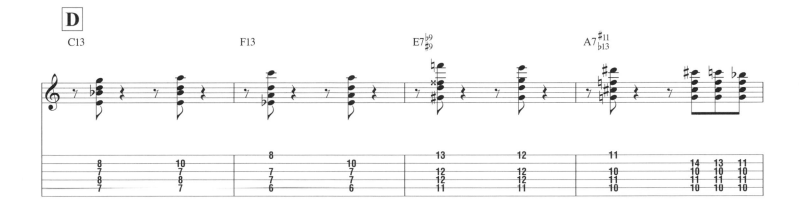

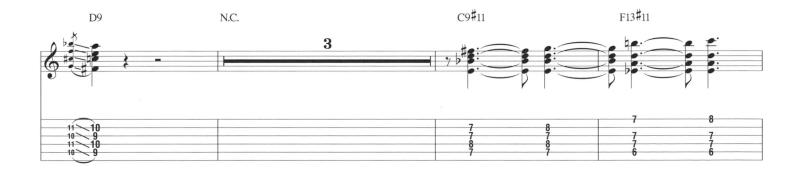

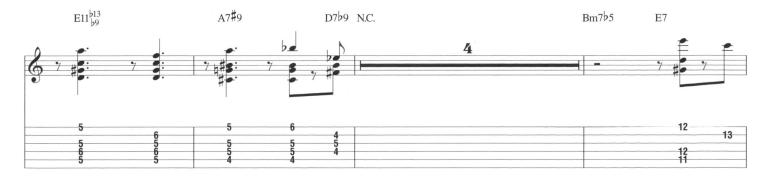

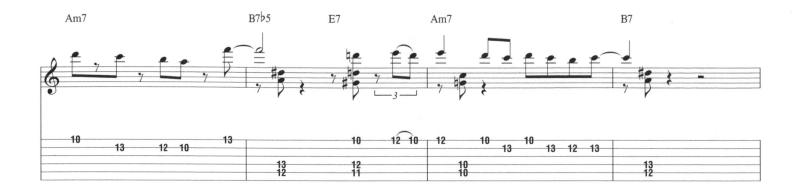

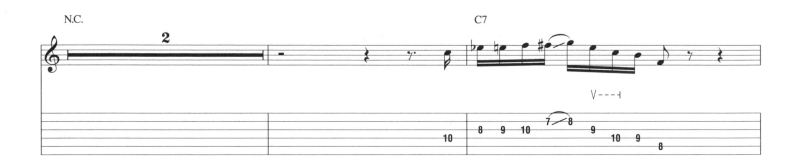

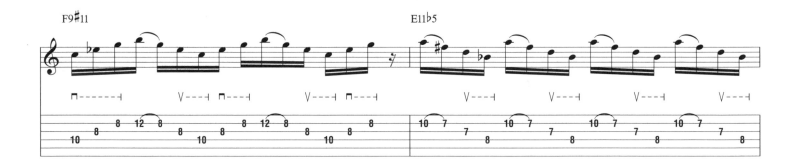

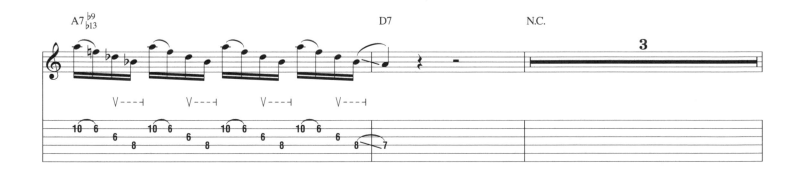

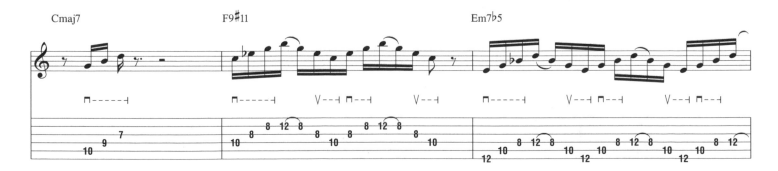

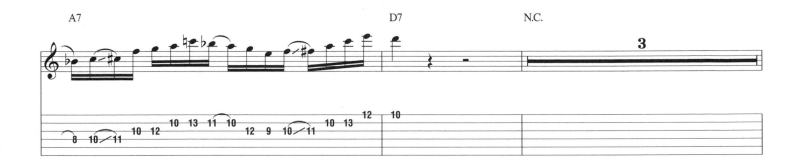

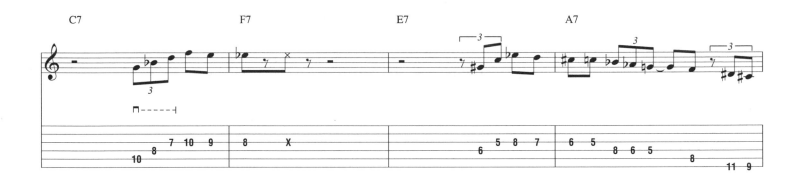

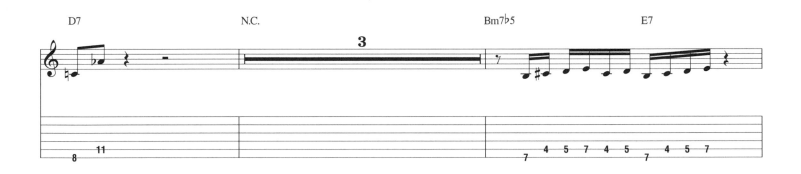

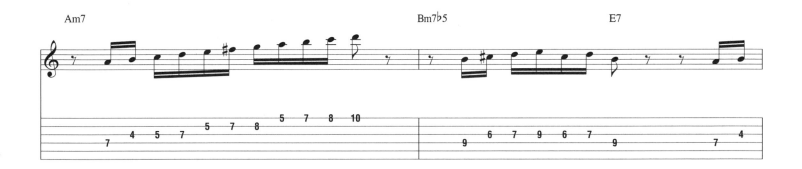

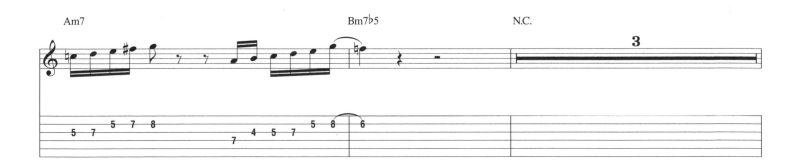

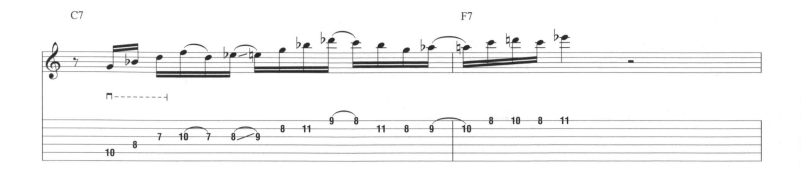

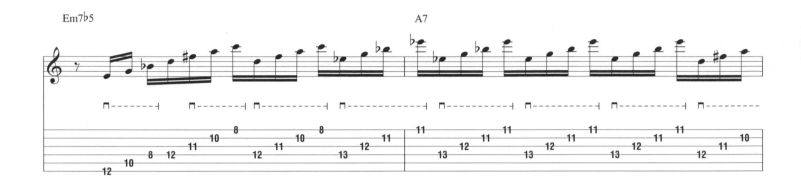

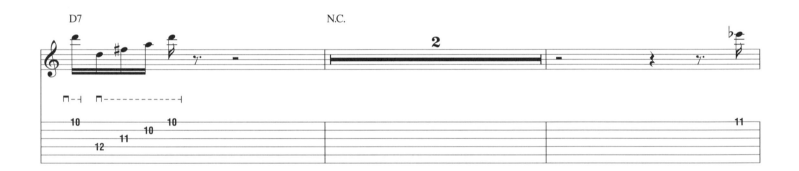

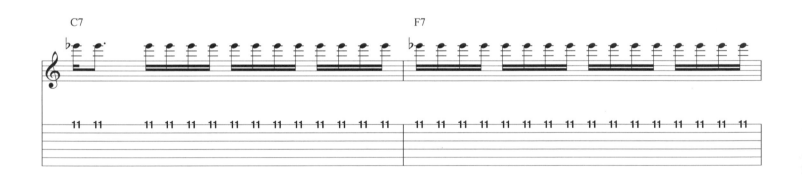

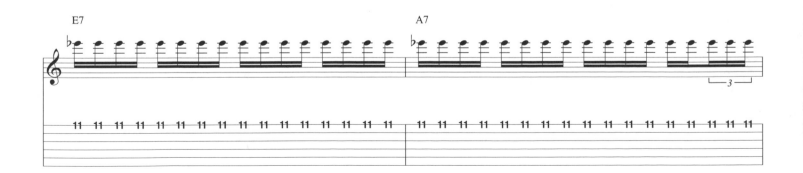

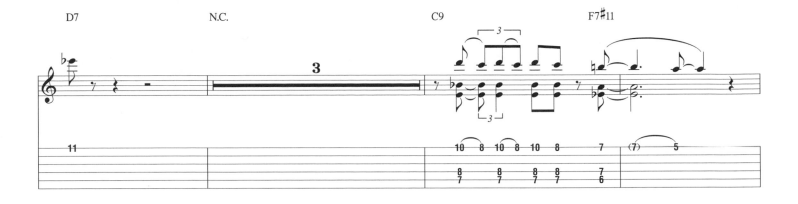

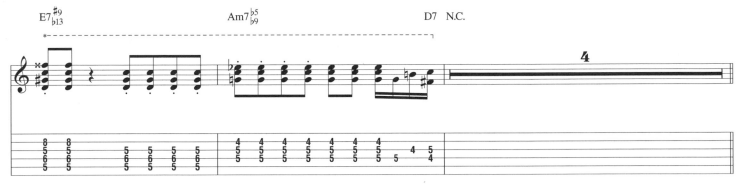

*Played as even eighth notes.

E

Double-time feel

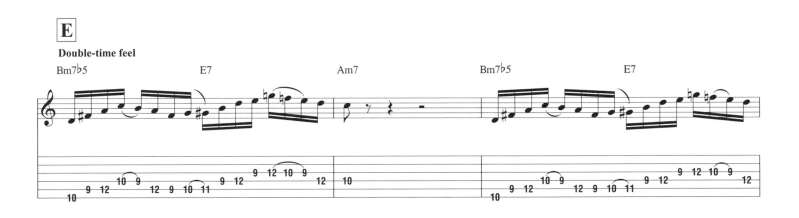

End double-time feel

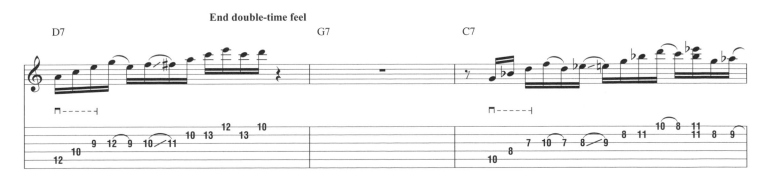

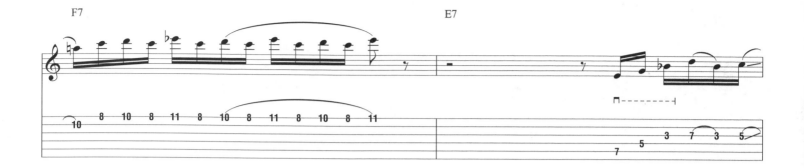

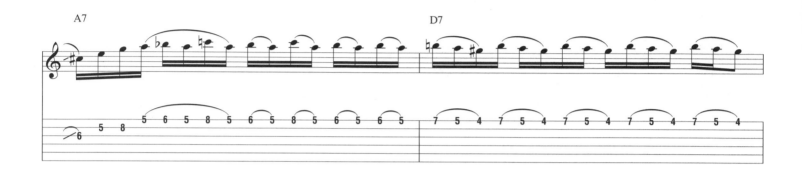

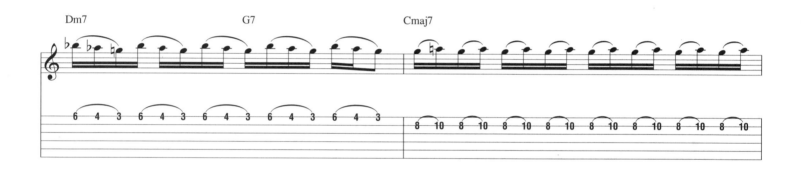

Double-time feel

Spoken: Uh,

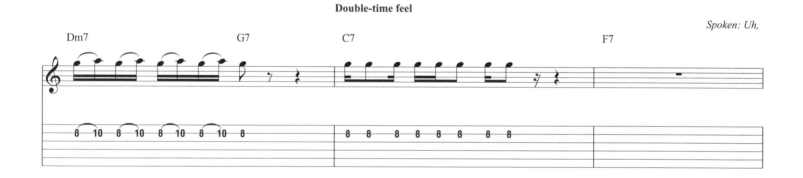

check it out.   Uh,   uh.

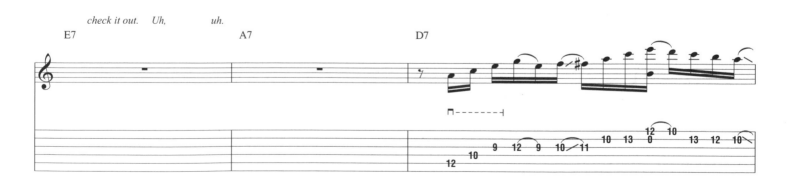

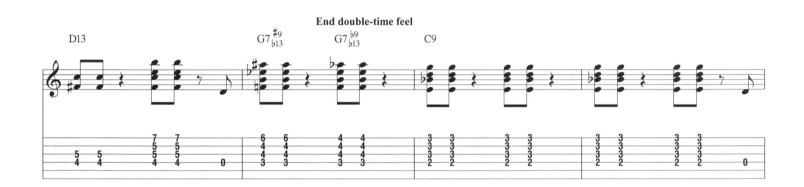

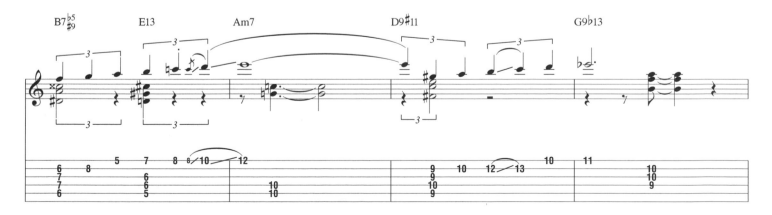

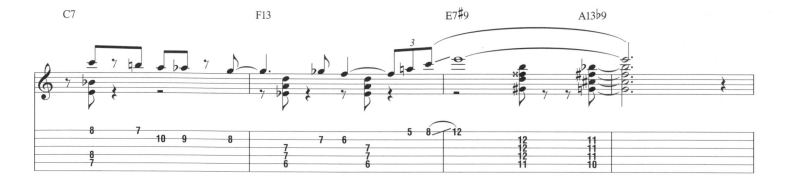

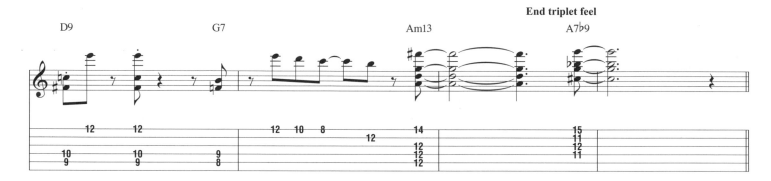

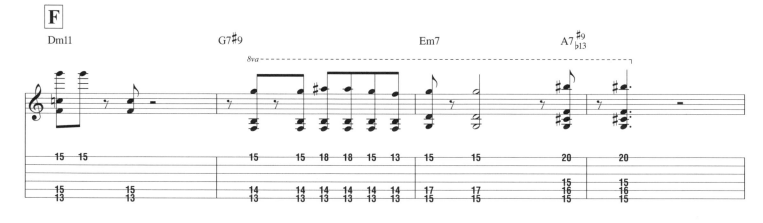

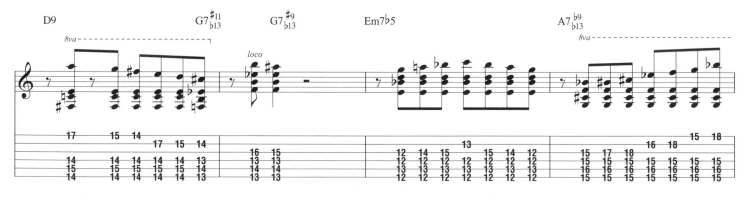

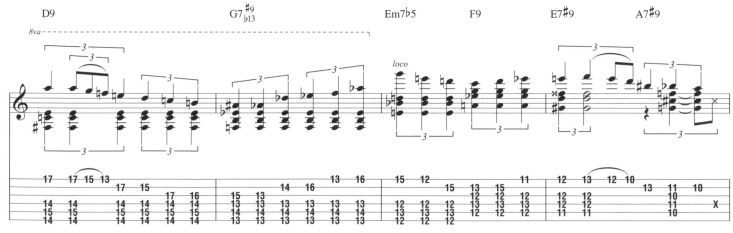

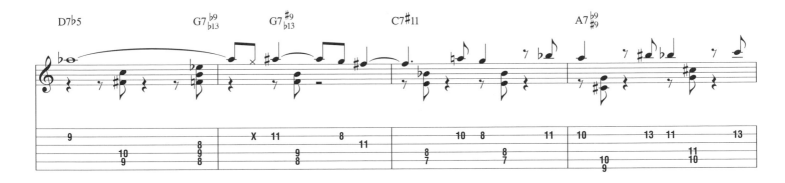

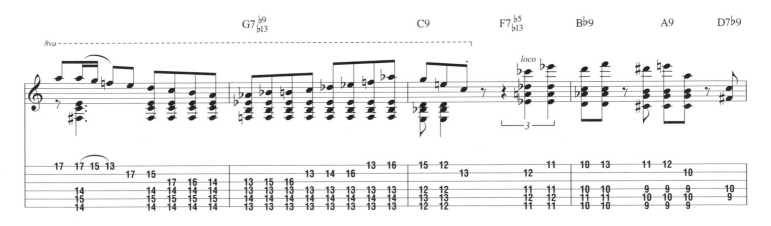

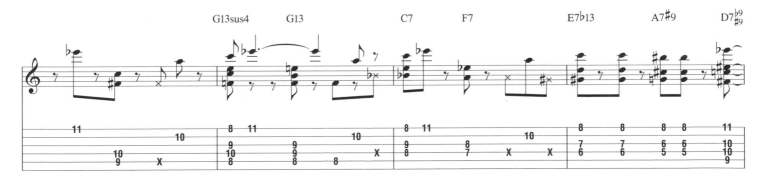

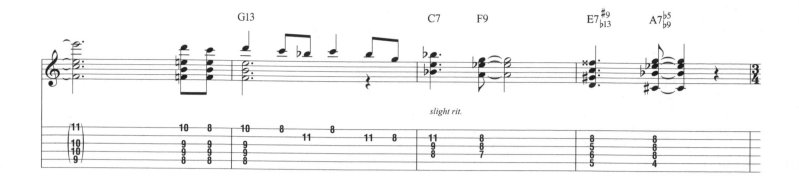

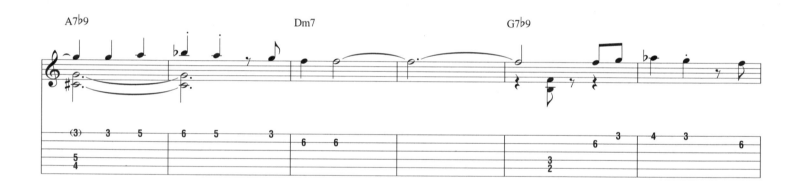

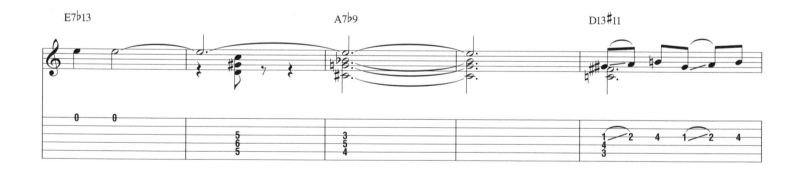

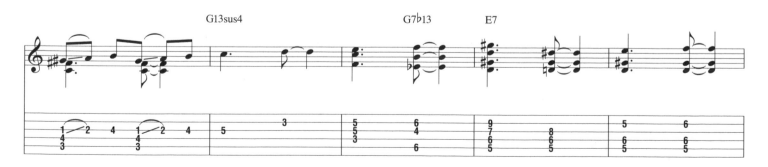

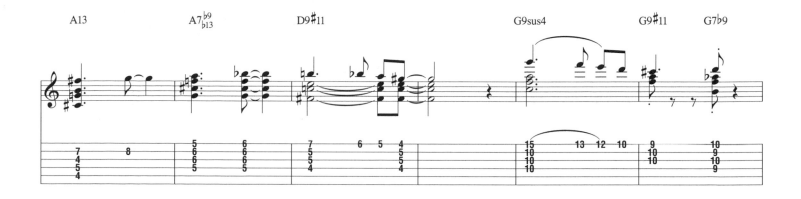

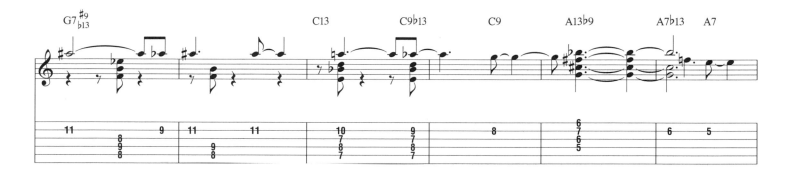

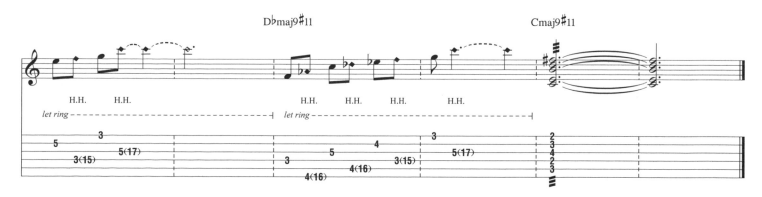

121

from *Five O'Clock Bells*
Visions
By McCoy Tyner

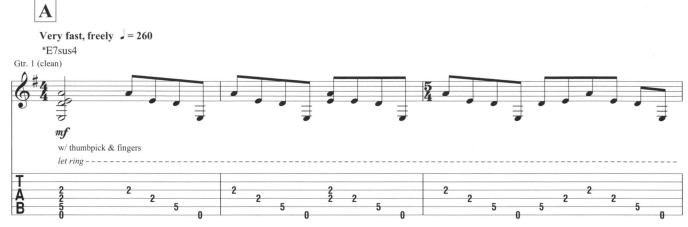

*Chord symbols reflect implied harmony.

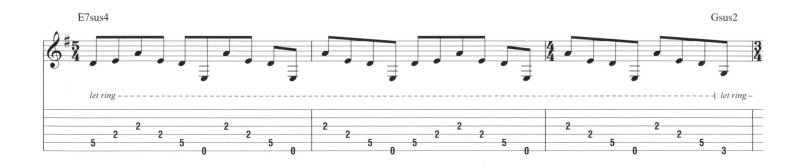

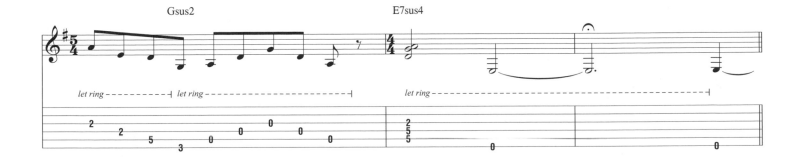

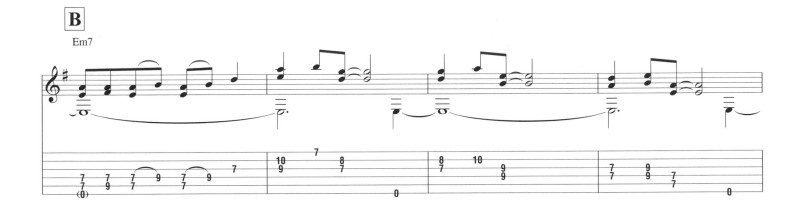

B

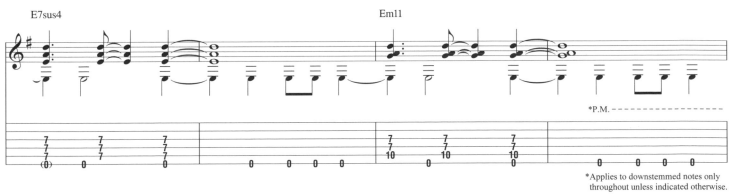

*Applies to downstemmed notes only
throughout unless indicated otherwise.

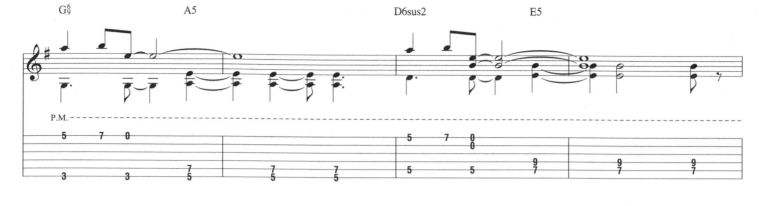

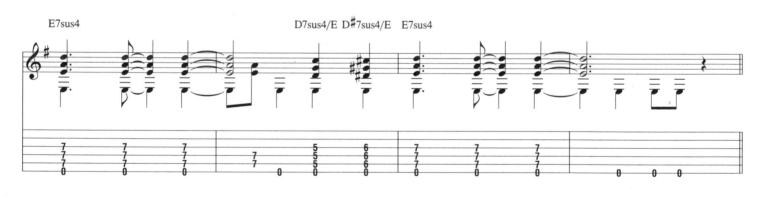

*Applies to all notes.

*Applies to all notes.

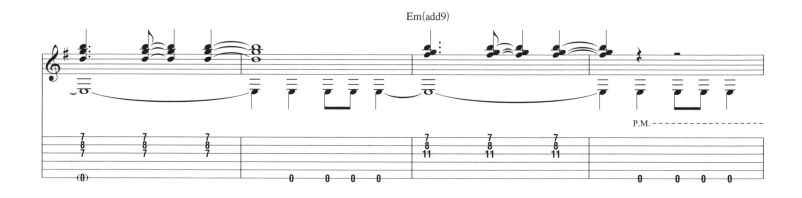

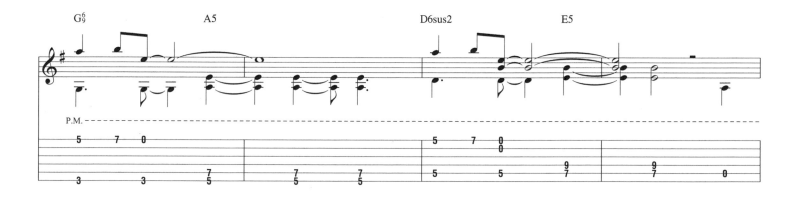

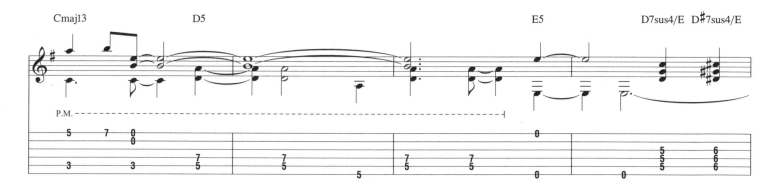

126

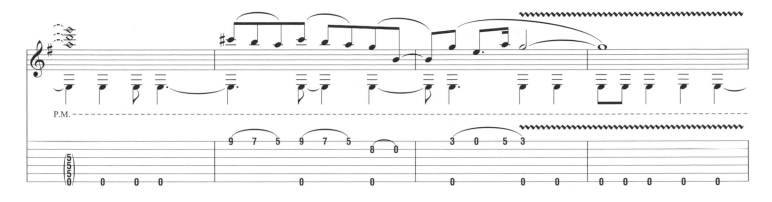

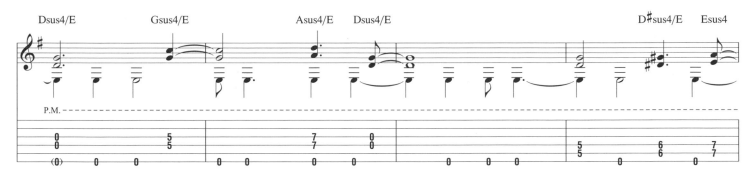

Dsus4/E   Gsus4/E   Asus4/E   Dsus4/E   D#sus4/E   Esus4

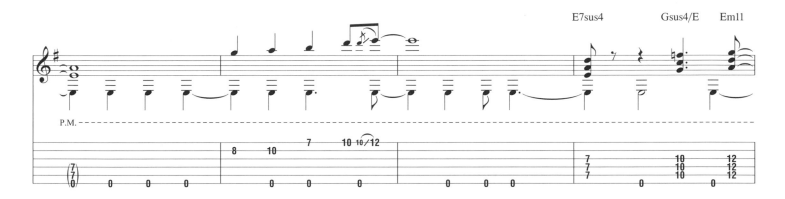

E7sus4   Gsus4/E   Em11

G#sus4/E   Gsus4/E

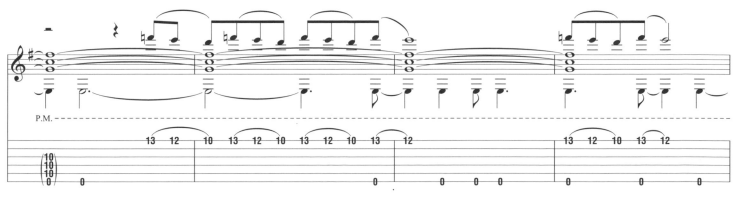

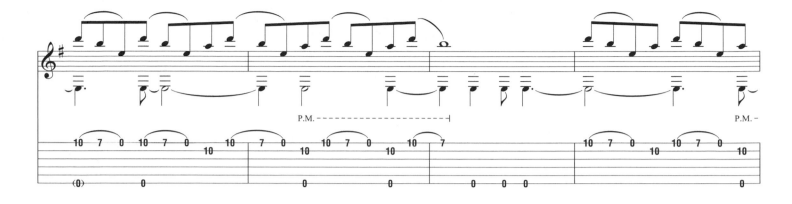

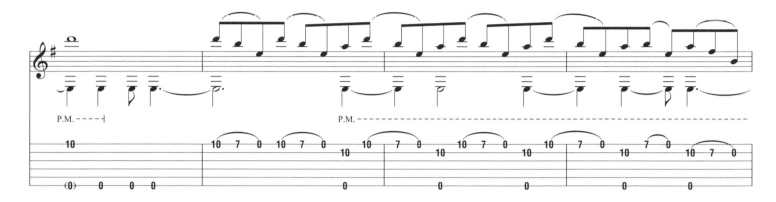

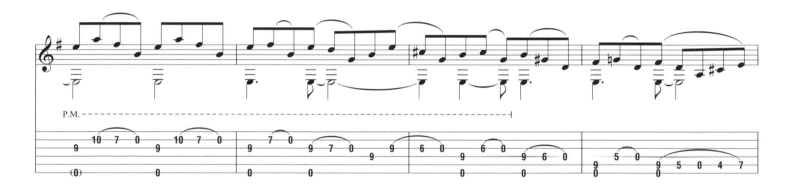

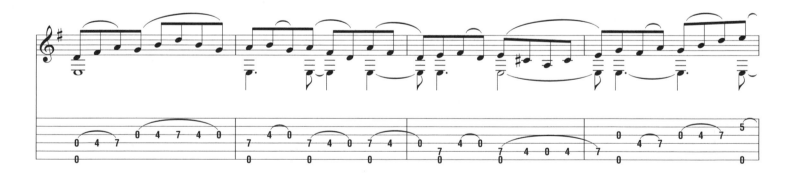

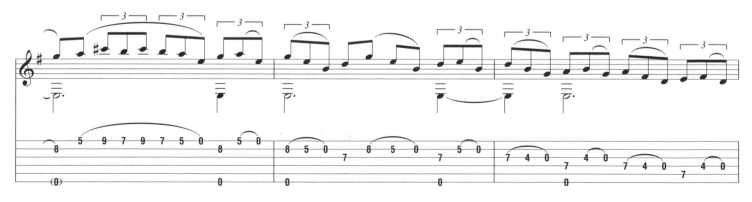

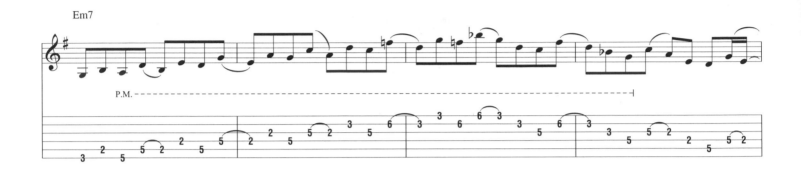

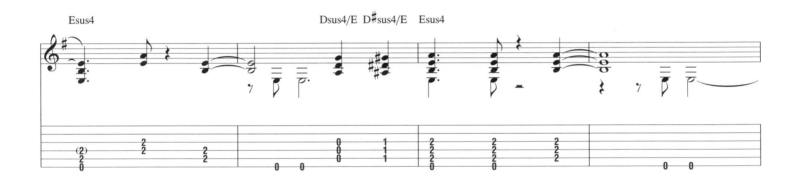

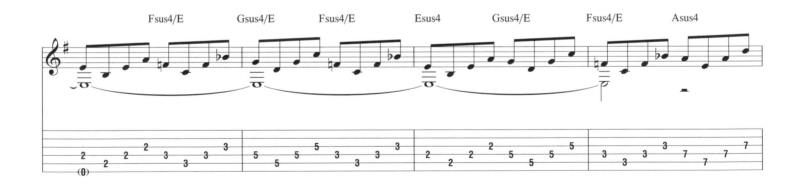

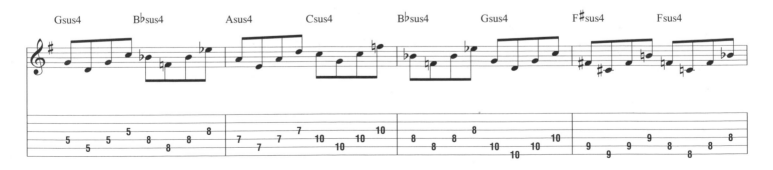

Esus4   Dsus4/E D♯sus4/E   Esus4   Dsus4/E D♯sus4/E

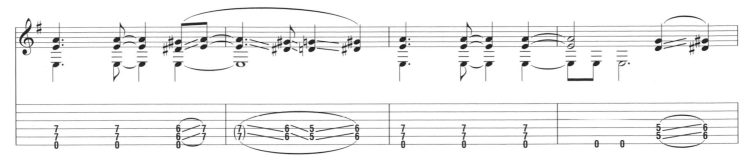

Esus4   D7sus4/E D♯sus4/E E7sus4

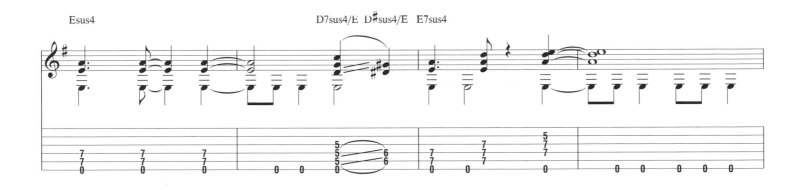

Em7

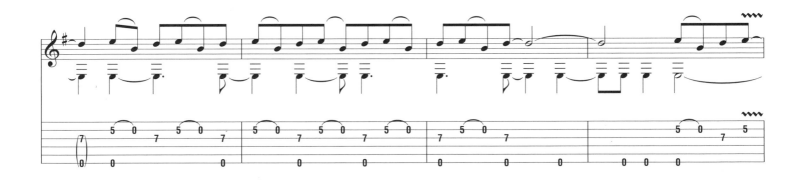

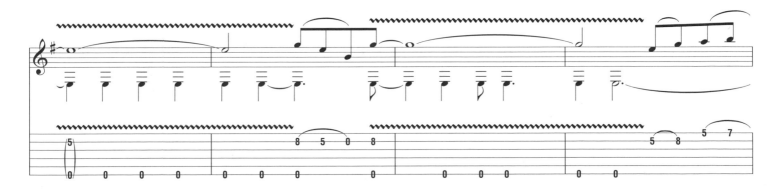

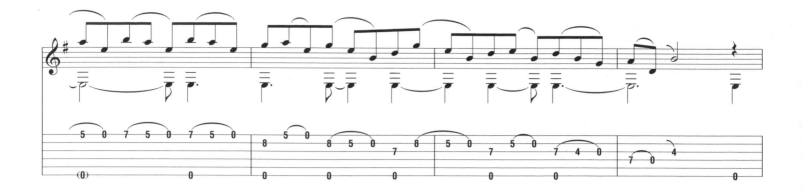

G13

F$\frac{9}{6}$#11

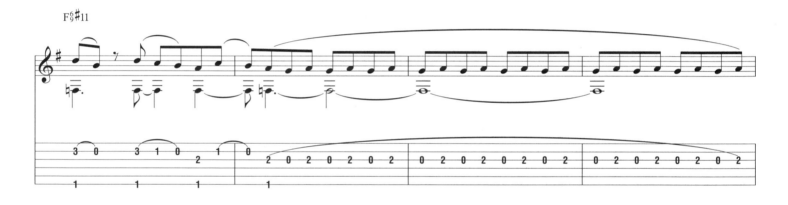

Esus4   **C7sus4/E**

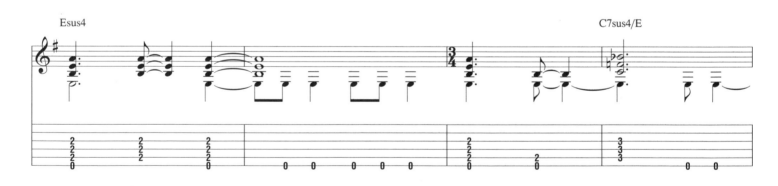

D7sus4/E   **F7sus4/E**   **E7sus4**   **D7sus4/E**   **C7sus4/E**

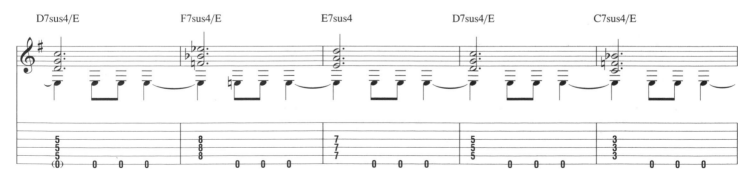

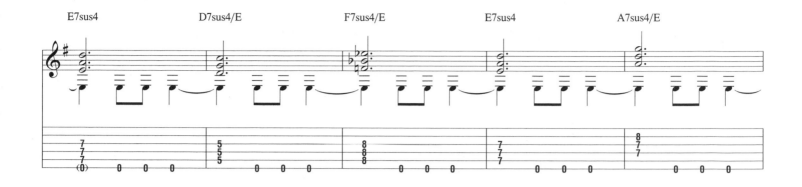

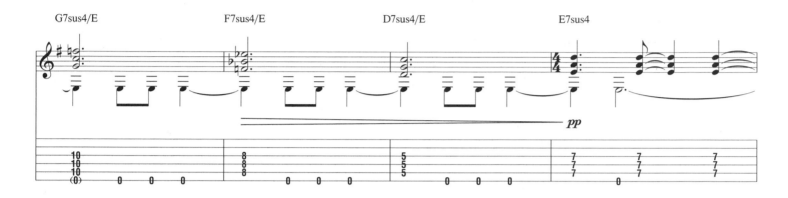

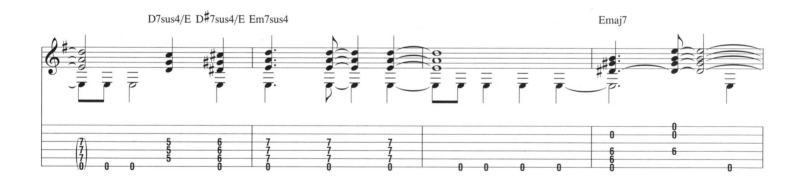

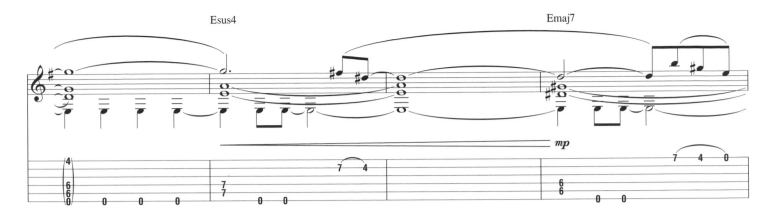

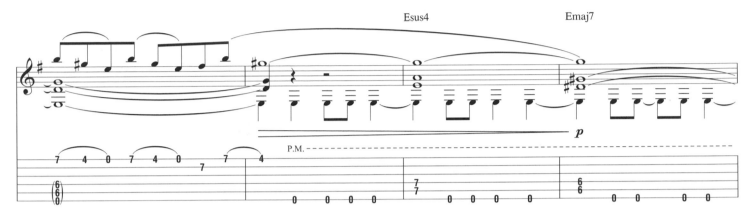

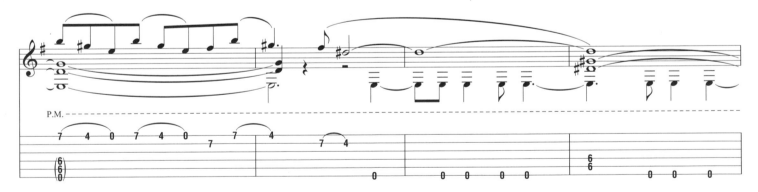

Esus4 Emaj7

Esus4 Emaj7

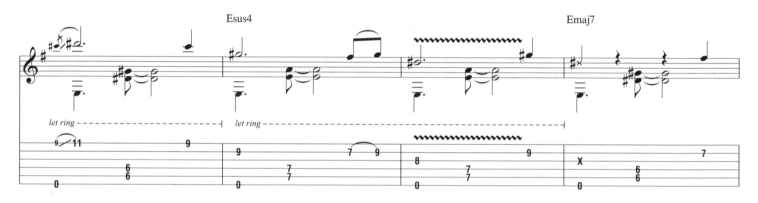

Esus4 Emaj7

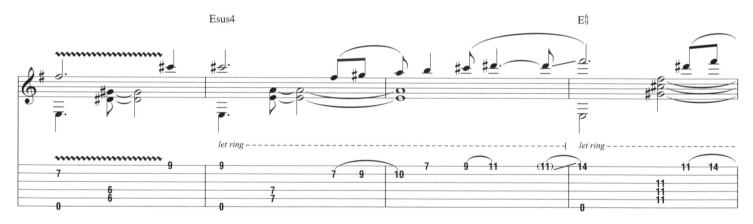

Esus4 E$^6_9$

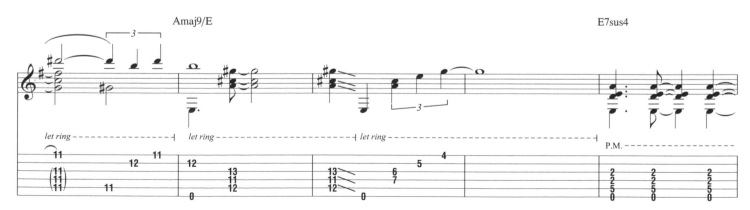

Amaj9/E E7sus4

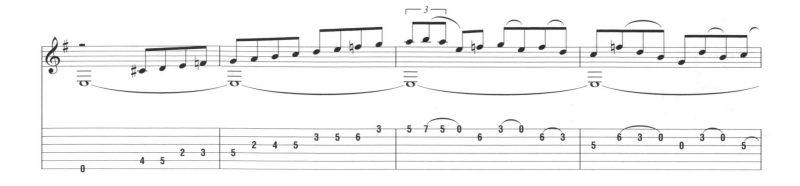

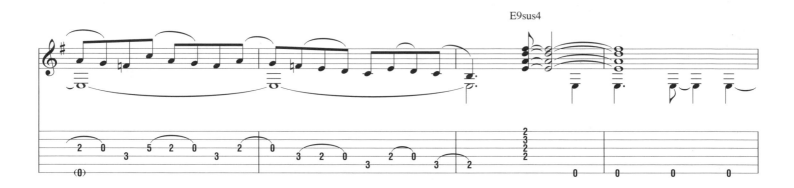

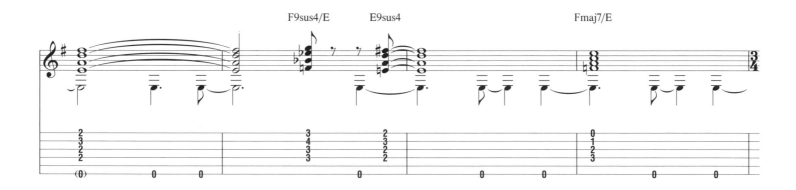

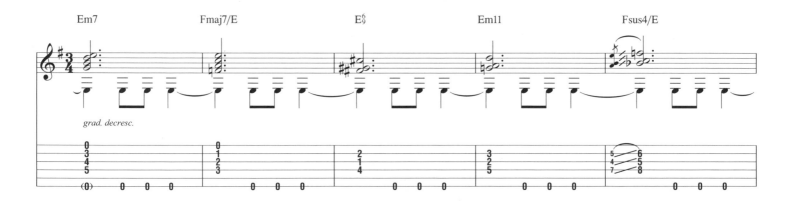

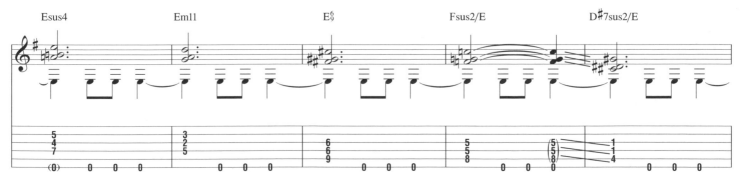

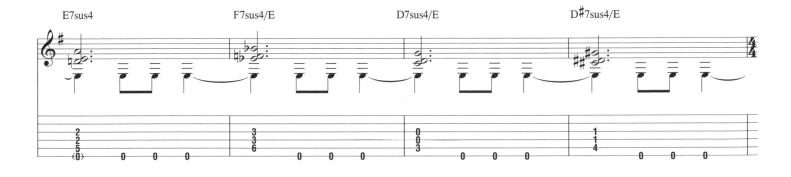

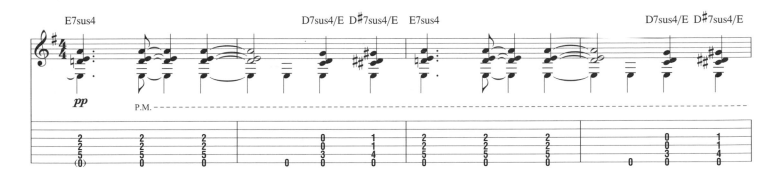

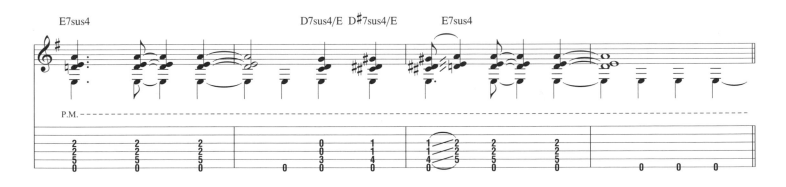

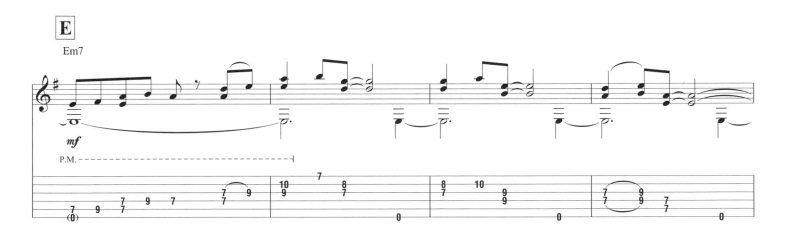

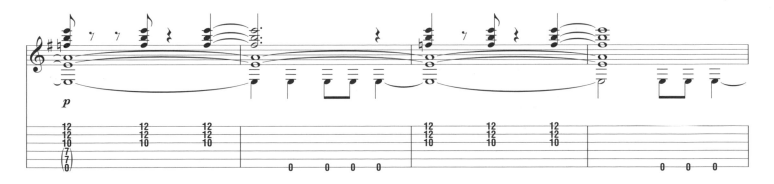

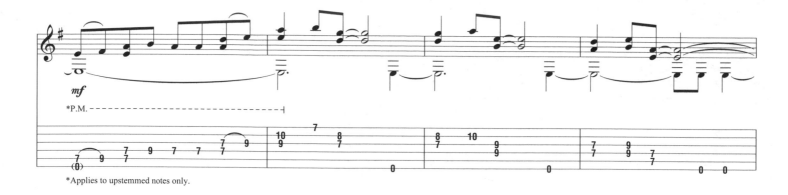

*Applies to upstemmed notes only.

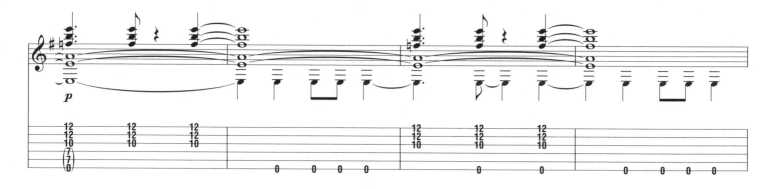

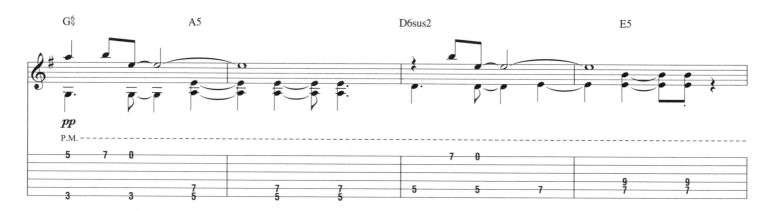

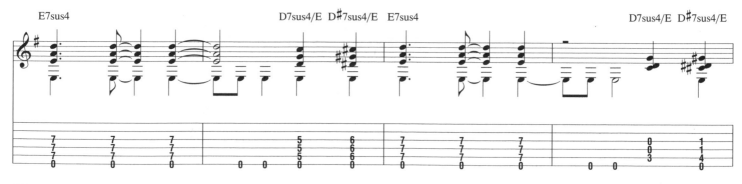

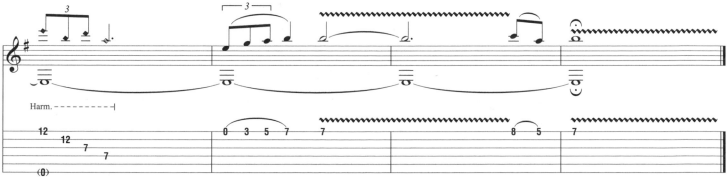

GUITAR NOTATION LEGEND

Guitar music can be notated three different ways: on a *musical staff*, in *tablature*, and in *rhythm slashes*.

RHYTHM SLASHES are written above the staff. Strum chords in the rhythm indicated. Use the chord diagrams found at the top of the first page of the transcription for the appropriate chord voicings. Round noteheads indicate single notes.

THE MUSICAL STAFF shows pitches and rhythms and is divided by bar lines into measures. Pitches are named after the first seven letters of the alphabet.

TABLATURE graphically represents the guitar fingerboard. Each horizontal line represents a string, and each number represents a fret.

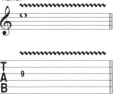

4th string, 2nd fret   1st & 2nd strings open, played together   open D chord

HALF-STEP BEND: Strike the note and bend up 1/2 step.

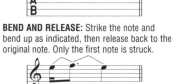

WHOLE-STEP BEND: Strike the note and bend up one step.

GRACE NOTE BEND: Strike the note and immediately bend up as indicated.

SLIGHT (MICROTONE) BEND: Strike the note and bend up 1/4 step.

BEND AND RELEASE: Strike the note and bend up as indicated, then release back to the original note. Only the first note is struck.

PRE-BEND: Bend the note as indicated, then strike it.

VIBRATO: The string is vibrated by rapidly bending and releasing the note with the fretting hand.

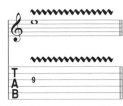

WIDE VIBRATO: The pitch is varied to a greater degree by vibrating with the fretting hand.

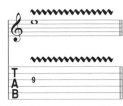

HAMMER-ON: Strike the first (lower) note with one finger, then sound the higher note (on the same string) with another finger by fretting it without picking.

PULL-OFF: Place both fingers on the notes to be sounded. Strike the first note and without picking, pull the finger off to sound the second (lower) note.

LEGATO SLIDE: Strike the first note and then slide the same fret-hand finger up or down to the second note. The second note is not struck.

SHIFT SLIDE: Same as legato slide, except the second note is struck.

TRILL: Very rapidly alternate between the notes indicated by continuously hammering on and pulling off.

TAPPING: Hammer ("tap") the fret indicated with the pick-hand index or middle finger and pull off to the note fretted by the fret hand.

NATURAL HARMONIC: Strike the note while the fret-hand lightly touches the string directly over the fret indicated.

PINCH HARMONIC: The note is fretted normally and a harmonic is produced by adding the edge of the thumb or the tip of the index finger of the pick hand to the normal pick attack.

PICK SCRAPE: The edge of the pick is rubbed down (or up) the string, producing a scratchy sound.

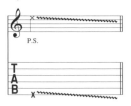

MUFFLED STRINGS: A percussive sound is produced by laying the fret hand across the string(s) without depressing, and striking them with the pick hand.

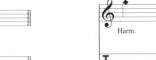

PALM MUTING: The note is partially muted by the pick hand lightly touching the string(s) just before the bridge.

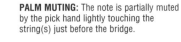
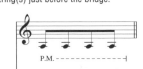

RAKE: Drag the pick across the strings indicated with a single motion.

TREMOLO PICKING: The note is picked as rapidly and continuously as possible.

VIBRATO BAR DIVE AND RETURN: The pitch of the note or chord is dropped a specified number of steps (in rhythm), then returned to the original pitch.

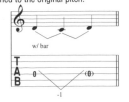

VIBRATO BAR SCOOP: Depress the bar just before striking the note, then quickly release the bar.

VIBRATO BAR DIP: Strike the note and then immediately drop a specified number of steps, then release back to the original pitch.

JAZZ GUITAR CHORD MELODY SOLOS

This series features chord melody arrangements in standard notation and tablature of songs for intermediate guitarists.

ALL-TIME STANDARDS `INCLUDES TAB`
27 songs, including: All of Me • Bewitched • Come Fly with Me • A Fine Romance • Georgia on My Mind • How High the Moon • I'll Never Smile Again • I've Got You Under My Skin • It's De-Lovely • It's Only a Paper Moon • My Romance • Satin Doll • The Surrey with the Fringe on Top • Yesterdays • and more.
00699757 Solo Guitar $14.99

CHRISTMAS CAROLS `INCLUDES TAB`
26 songs, including: Auld Lang Syne • Away in a Manger • Deck the Hall • God Rest Ye Merry, Gentlemen • Good King Wenceslas • Here We Come A-Wassailing • It Came upon the Midnight Clear • Joy to the World • O Holy Night • O Little Town of Bethlehem • Silent Night • Toyland • We Three Kings of Orient Are • and more.
00701697 Solo Guitar $12.99

DISNEY SONGS `INCLUDES TAB`
27 songs, including: Beauty and the Beast • Can You Feel the Love Tonight • Candle on the Water • Colors of the Wind • A Dream Is a Wish Your Heart Makes • Heigh-Ho • Some Day My Prince Will Come • Under the Sea • When You Wish upon a Star • A Whole New World (Aladdin's Theme) • Zip-A-Dee-Doo-Dah • and more.
00701902 Solo Guitar $14.99

DUKE ELLINGTON `INCLUDES TAB`
25 songs, including: C-Jam Blues • Caravan • Do Nothin' Till You Hear from Me • Don't Get Around Much Anymore • I Got It Bad and That Ain't Good • I'm Just a Lucky So and So • In a Sentimental Mood • It Don't Mean a Thing (If It Ain't Got That Swing) • Mood Indigo • Perdido • Prelude to a Kiss • Satin Doll • and more.
00700636 Solo Guitar $12.99

FAVORITE STANDARDS `INCLUDES TAB`
27 songs, including: All the Way • Autumn in New York • Blue Skies • Cheek to Cheek • Don't Get Around Much Anymore • How Deep Is the Ocean • I'll Be Seeing You • Isn't It Romantic? • It Could Happen to You • The Lady Is a Tramp • Moon River • Speak Low • Take the "A" Train • Willow Weep for Me • Witchcraft • and more.
00699756 Solo Guitar $14.99

FINGERPICKING JAZZ STANDARDS `INCLUDES TAB`
15 songs: Autumn in New York • Body and Soul • Can't Help Lovin' Dat Man • Easy Living • A Fine Romance • Have You Met Miss Jones? • I'm Beginning to See the Light • It Could Happen to You • My Romance • Stella by Starlight • Tangerine • The Very Thought of You • The Way You Look Tonight • When Sunny Gets Blue • Yesterdays.
00699840 Solo Guitar $7.99

JAZZ BALLADS `INCLUDES TAB`
27 songs, including: Body and Soul • Darn That Dream • Easy to Love (You'd Be So Easy to Love) • Here's That Rainy Day • In a Sentimental Mood • Misty • My Foolish Heart • My Funny Valentine • The Nearness of You • Stella by Starlight • Time After Time • The Way You Look Tonight • When Sunny Gets Blue • and more.
00699755 Solo Guitar $14.99

JAZZ CLASSICS `INCLUDES TAB`
27 songs, including: Blue in Green • Bluesette • Bouncing with Bud • Cast Your Fate to the Wind • Con Alma • Doxy • Epistrophy • Footprints • Giant Steps • Invitation • Lullaby of Birdland • Lush Life • A Night in Tunisia • Nuages • Ruby, My Dear • St. Thomas • Stolen Moments • Waltz for Debby • Yardbird Suite • and more.
00699758 Solo Guitar $14.99

Prices, content, and availability subject to change without notice. | Disney characters and artwork ©Disney Enterprises, Inc.

> **"Well-crafted arrangements that sound great and are still accessible to most players."**
> – *Guitar Edge* magazine

HAL•LEONARD®
www.halleonard.com

IMPROVE YOUR IMPROV
AND OTHER JAZZ TECHNIQUES WITH BOOKS FROM HAL LEONARD

JAZZ GUITAR

HAL LEONARD GUITAR METHOD
by Jeff Schroedl

The Hal Leonard Jazz Guitar Method is your complete guide to learning jazz guitar. This book uses real jazz songs to teach the basics of accompanying and improvising jazz guitar in the style of Wes Montgomery, Joe Pass, Tal Farlow, Charlie Christian, Pat Martino, Barney Kessel, Jim Hall, and many others.
00695359 Book/CD Pack...............................$19.99

AMAZING PHRASING

50 WAYS TO IMPROVE YOUR
IMPROVISATIONAL SKILLS • *by Tom Kolb*

This book/CD pack explores all the main components necessary for crafting well-balanced rhythmic and melodic phrases. It also explains how these phrases are put together to form cohesive solos. Many styles are covered – rock, blues, jazz, fusion, country, Latin, funk and more – and all of the concepts are backed up with musical examples.
00695583 Book/CD Pack...............................$19.95

BEST OF JAZZ GUITAR
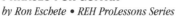

by Wolf Marshall • Signature Licks

In this book/CD pack, Wolf Marshall provides a hands-on analysis of 10 of the most frequently played tunes in the jazz genre, as played by the leading guitarists of all time. Each selection includes technical analysis and performance notes, biographical sketches, and authentic matching audio with backing tracks.
00695586 Book/CD Pack...............................$24.95

CHORD-MELODY PHRASES FOR GUITAR

by Ron Eschete • REH ProLessons Series

Expand your chord-melody chops with these outstanding jazz phrases! This book covers: chord substitutions, chromatic movements, contrary motion, pedal tones, inner-voice movements, reharmonization techniques, and much more. Includes standard notation and tab, and a CD.
00695628 Book/CD Pack...............................$17.99

CHORDS FOR JAZZ GUITAR

THE COMPLETE GUIDE TO COMPING,
CHORD MELODY AND CHORD SOLOING • *by Charlton Johnson*

This book/CD pack will teach you how to play jazz chords all over the fretboard in a variety of styles and progressions. It covers: voicings, progressions, jazz chord theory, comping, chord melody, chord soloing, voice leading and many more topics. The CD includes 98 full-band demo tracks. No tablature.
00695706 Book/CD Pack...............................$19.95

CRASH COURSE ON JAZZ GUITAR VOICINGS

THE ESSENTIAL GUIDE FOR ALL GUITARISTS
by Hugh Burns • Artemis Editions

This ultimate beginner's guide to jazz guitar covers: jazz harmony explained simply, easy essential jazz shapes to get you playing right away, classic jazz progressions, vamps, turnarounds and substitutions and more.
00695815 Book/CD Pack............................... $9.95

FRETBOARD ROADMAPS – JAZZ GUITAR

THE ESSENTIAL GUITAR PATTERNS
THAT ALL THE PROS KNOW AND USE • *by Fred Sokolow*

This book/CD pack will get guitarists playing lead & rhythm anywhere on the fretboard, in any key! It teaches a variety of lead guitar styles using moveable patterns, double-note licks, sliding pentatonics and more, through easy-to-follow diagrams and instructions. The CD includes 54 full-demo tracks.
00695354 Book/CD Pack...............................$14.95

JAZZ IMPROVISATION FOR GUITAR

by Les Wise • REH ProLessons Series

This book/CD will allow you to make the transition from playing disjointed scales and arpeggios to playing melodic jazz solos that maintain continuity and interest for the listener. Topics covered include: tension and resolution, major scale, melodic minor scale, and harmonic minor scale patterns, common licks and substitution techniques, creating altered tension, and more! Features standard notation and tab, and a CD.
00695657 Book/CD Pack...............................$16.95

JAZZ RHYTHM GUITAR

THE COMPLETE GUIDE
by Jack Grassel

This book/CD pack will help rhythm guitarists better understand: chord symbols and voicings, comping styles and patterns, equipment, accessories and set-up, the fingerboard, chord theory, and much more. The accompanying CD includes 74 full-band tracks.
00695654 Book/CD Pack...............................$19.95

JAZZ SOLOS FOR GUITAR
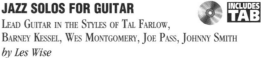

LEAD GUITAR IN THE STYLES OF TAL FARLOW,
BARNEY KESSEL, WES MONTGOMERY, JOE PASS, JOHNNY SMITH
by Les Wise

Examine the solo concepts of the masters with this book including phrase-by-phrase performance notes, tips on arpeggio substitution, scale substitution, tension and resolution, jazz-blues, chord soloing, and more. The CD includes full demonstration and rhythm-only tracks.
00695447 Book/CD Pack...............................$17.95

101 MUST-KNOW JAZZ LICKS

A QUICK, EASY REFERENCE GUIDE
FOR ALL GUITARISTS • *by Wolf Marshall*

Here are 101 definitive licks, plus a demonstration CD, from every major jazz guitar style, neatly organized into easy-to-use categories. They're all here: swing and pre-bop, bebop, post-bop modern jazz, hard bop and cool jazz, modal jazz, soul jazz and postmodern jazz. Includes an introduction, tips for using the book/CD, and a list of suggested recordings.
00695433 Book/CD Pack...............................$17.95

SWING AND BIG BAND GUITAR

FOUR-TO-THE-BAR COMPING IN THE STYLE OF
FREDDIE GREEN • *by Charlton Johnson*

This unique package teaches the essentials of swing and big band styles, including chord voicings, inversions, substitutions; time and groove, reading charts, chord reduction, and expansion; sample songs, patterns, progressions, and exercises; chord reference library; and a CD with over 50 full-demo examples. Uses chord grids – no tablature.
00695147 Book/CD Pack...............................$19.99

FOR MORE INFORMATION, SEE YOUR LOCAL MUSIC DEALER,
OR WRITE TO:

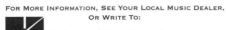

HAL•LEONARD®
CORPORATION
7777 W. BLUEMOUND RD. P.O. BOX 13819 MILWAUKEE, WI 53213

Visit Hal Leonard Online at **www.halleonard.com**

Prices, contents and availability
subject to change without notice.